Foreword

◉ **Supermarine Spitfire Mk VII, MD139, ON•W, of No.124 Squadron, flown by F/O W. Hibbert, RAF Bradwell Bay, June 1944**
Medium Sea Grey and PRU Blue finish with Type B roundels on fuselage and upper surfaces of wings only; full invasion stripes that cover the serial on the fuselage

Airframe Extra No.1
D-Day to VE-Day: The Battle Over Europe

First published in 2015 by Valiant Wings Publishing Ltd
8 West Grove, Bedford, Bedfordshire, MK40 4BT, UK
+44 (0)1234 273434
valiant-wings@btconnect.com
www.valiant-wings.co.uk

© Richard A. Franks 2015
© Richard J. Caruana – Colour Profiles
© Steve A. Evans 2015 (Section 2b)
© Libor Jekl 2015 (Section 2a)
© Dani Zamarbide 2015 (Section 2c – P-47D)
© Alan Bottoms 2015 (Section 2c – Spitfire)

The right of Richard A. Franks to be identified as the author of this work has been asserted in accordance with sections 77 and 78 of the Copyright Designs and Patents Act, 1988.

The 'Airframe Extra' brand, along with the concept of the series, are the copyright of Richard A. Franks as defined by the Copyright Designs and Patents Act, 1988 and are used by Valiant Wings Publishing Ltd by agreement with the copyright holder.

All rights reserved. No part of this publication may be reproduced or transmitted in any form or by any means, electronic or mechanical, including photocopy, recording, or any other information storage and retrieval system, without permission in writing from the publishers.

ISBN 978-0-9930908-1-3

Acknowledgements
The author would like to give a special word of thanks to Alan Bottoms, Steve A. Evans, Libor Jekl and Dani Zamarbide for their excellent builds featured in this special and to Richard J, Caruana for his superb artwork.

Note
There are many different ways of writing aircraft designation, however for consistency throughout this title we have used one style for each combatant nation, e.g. Me 109G-10, Me 262B-1a/U1 (Luftwaffe), Mk Ib, Mk Vc (RAF; the Arabic numbering system [Mk 1, Mk 5] was only adopted in 1948) and P-51D, P-47D (USAAF) etc.

Cover
The cover art depicts a Bf 109K-4 of JG4 in a scheme typical of that applied to their machines in 1944. The image is based on the accounts of the interception of USAAF B-17s by JG 4 on the 11th September 1944. ©Jerry Boucher 2015

Welcome to the first title in our new series in which we look at key moments and anniversaries in aviation combat history. *Airframe Extra* has been created for the aircraft modeller; we know that many of you like to model on historical themes. We aim to provide the inspiration for you to create a collection that commemorates a particular event. Equally, if there is one set of combatants or one individual aircraft that appeals, we believe that you'll find them amongst these pages.

The historical element provides the modelling context and has been written by our series editor, Richard A. Franks. Richard has been an innovative aviation author for over seventeen years with over thirty books under his belt. He has been the creative driving force behind Valiant Wings' book titles since our inception.

No book for aircraft modellers is complete without colour profiles – Richard J. Caruana's work is internationally acclaimed and has been gracing the pages of our books over the past five years. Always popular, sometimes courting debate, his profiles have enabled modellers to create subjects in special schemes. You should find plenty from the 81 profiles on offer here.

There are seven superb step-by-step model builds from Daniel Zamarbide, Steve A. Evans, Libor Jekl and Alan Bottoms; all modellers at the top of their game *and* with the ability to make their skills and techniques available to all. We are confident that having read about their experience you'll be inspired to try new techniques and take your skills to the next level.

We hope you enjoy reading *D-Day To VE Day* and have it by you on your workbench; that in so doing you enjoy creating small monuments to a remarkable generation of young men, irrespective of the colours under which they flew.

Many thanks for buying our books.

Mark Peacock – *Publisher*

Content

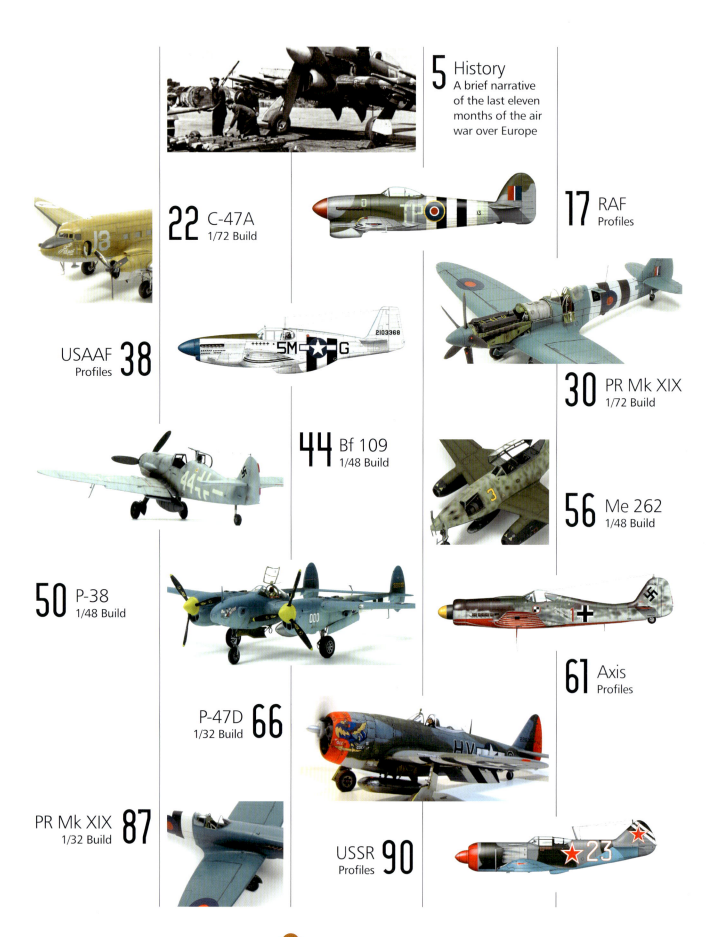

5 History
A brief narrative of the last eleven months of the air war over Europe

22 C-47A
1/72 Build

17 RAF Profiles

38 USAAF Profiles

30 PR Mk XIX
1/72 Build

44 Bf 109
1/48 Build

56 Me 262
1/48 Build

50 P-38
1/48 Build

61 Axis Profiles

66 P-47D
1/32 Build

87 PR Mk XIX
1/32 Build

90 USSR Profiles

History

Much has been written over the intervening 70 years about the end of the War in Europe and the events that took place from the Allied invasion in June 1944 through to the capitulation of the Nazi regime in May 1945. Although it is not my intention to go over events in detail it is good to understand the situation overall both from the Allied and Axis sides, and to do this the only real way is to look at key events in chronological order, instead of a rambling historical narrative. To that end what follows is such a list, with details of all the main events as they occurred. From June 1944 the Air War was, from the Allied perspective, a tactical one in support of the liberating forces on the ground, whilst the Axis were on the defensive trying to stem the advance of the Allies.

Prelude

Before we start at D-Day, you have to understand that the whole idea of a combined Allied invasion of Europe had been in the mind of the Allied commanders for many years. In May 1942 a special unit had been set up and this department, headed by Major George Yool, moved from RAF Medmenham, where the Central Interpretation Unit was situated, to Norfolk House, off St. James' Square in London as a new section of the Army Photographic Interpretations Service. His team was to begin searching for potential landing beaches along the entire coast of occupied Europe, from Den Helder in northern Holland to south–west France and the Spanish borders, for up to 30 miles inland. The RAF PR units in their modified Spitfires undertook systematic photography of every port and harbour in northern France and the Low Countries to determine the defences in each area and thus identify a potential landing area. The disaster of the Dieppe raid in August 1942 proved that the equipment and knowledge that the Allies had of Europe was insufficient to allow a massive landing to be successful. Much of the failure of the raid was put down to poor intelligence gained from aerial photography, with the interpreters failing to note such things as gun emplacements and the strength of defending forces. This was mainly due to the fact that aerial photography had been used up to this point for identifying targets for bombing and assessing the effects of such raids, so the interpreters only had experience in these elements and that is why the Army branch was established, to look at the specific information needs of ground forces. This was to

Final preparations before RAF Dakotas begin their journey towards the landing grounds of Normandy, loaded with troops and equipment, or with gliders on tow
(©R.J. Caruana Archives)

by Richard A. Franks

play an important part in the invasion of North Africa, Operation Torch, in November 1942 and in the preparation for the invasion of Sicily in July 1943, where the Photo-Interpreters learned to do such things as measure the angle of a beach, or to identify mines and other obstacles. The decision to launch the Allied liberation of Europe was made at the Quadrant Conference in August 1943 and although the shortest crossing to the Pas de Calais was the obvious choice, the German's had heavily fortified the ports in this region having also identified them as the most likely landing zones, so the Normandy beaches were chosen as the best option and the invasion was set for the 1st May 1944. Once the two Allied commanders, General Eisenhower and Montgomery, saw the plans, though, they both agreed that the ground forces needed to be increased by five divisions, whilst the air force had to be increased by three. The result of this was that the increased equipment required, especially the landing craft, meant a delay until June 1944.

Nice shot of a Horsa being towed by a Halifax towards the Normandy coast. Note that both machines only have the D-Day stripes around the rear fuselage

June
1944

Note: In the build-up to D-Day the RAF and USAAF photo-reconnaissance units undertake 3,200 sorties from April 1944 all along the French coast, photographing all military installations and equipment as well as the rail and road infrastructure. In all 1.2 million photographs were taken and this was supported by over 10 million holiday photographs and maps donated by the British public after a BBC appeal.

1st June
▶ D-Day: The British Broadcasting Company (BBC) transmits the first line of the poem Chanson d'automne by Paul Verlaine, this being a pre-arranged code to notify the French Resistance that the invasion of Europe was imminent.
RAF & USAAF: A Combined Air Transport Command Room (CATOR) is established at RAF Stanmore to control the use of USAAF and RAF transport aircraft for supply by air.
▶ RAF: The RAF's Balkan Air Force (AVM W. Elliott) is formed to provide support for Marshal Tito's Yugoslavian partisans.

2nd June
▶ D-Day: In readiness for liberation, a provisional French government is established in London.

3rd June
▶ RAF & USAAF: Instructions are issued to apply 18in wide stripes (three white and two black) around each wing positioned 6in inboard of the underwing national insignia plus similar bands around the rear fuselage of all troop carrying aircraft.

An important element of the air armada put together for Operation Overlord consisted of target-towing transports, of which the Stirling featured prominently (©R.J. Caruana Archives)

4th June 4
▶ RAF: The bombing campaign against the coast gun batteries on the northern coast of France continues with 243 heavy bombers and 16 Mosquitos attacking four sites, three of which are deception targets in the Pas de Calais area, whilst the fourth is a battery at Maisy in Normandy between what will become Omaha and Utah beaches.
▶ RAF & USAAF: Instructions are issued to apply 18in wide stripes (three white and two black) around each wing positioned 6in inboard of the underwing national insignial plus similar bands around the rear fuselage of all fighter and bomber aircraft.
▶ Italy: Rome is liberated by Allied forces; this is the first Axis capital to fall.

5th June
▶ D-Day: Invasion scheduled to take place, but poor weather conditions lead the Supreme Commander of the Allied Forces, General Eisenhower, to postpone the offensive for 24 hours after receiving news from Group Captain James Stagg that the weather will briefly improve over the English Channel.
▶ D-Day: Royal Navy minesweepers start to clear a lane from the UK to France in readiness for the invasion fleet.
▶ D-Day: At 10:15p.m GNT, the BBC transmits the second line of Chanson d'automne, which tells the French Resistance that the invasion of Europe is about to begin.
▶ RAF & USAAF: Heavy and medium bombers drop more than 5,000 tons of bombs on German gun positions along the Normandy coast in preparation for the invasion.
▶ RAF & USAAF: Operation Tonga: Just before midnight the Allied invasion of north–west Europe (Operation Overlord) commences with British and American paratroop divisions being dropped behind enemy lines in Normandy by over 1,200 RAF and USAAF aircraft.

6th June
▶ D-Day: Over 132,000 Allied troops are landed on five beaches (Sword, Gold [British], Juno [Canadian] and Omaha and Utah [American]) in Normandy in northern France, along with a further 24,000 paratroopers dropped further inland.
▶ D-Day: The first infantry comes ashore at 06:30am, just five minutes after the 40 minutes naval bombardment has ceased.
▶ RAF: 5,656 sorties flown in support of the landing with the loss of 113 aircraft.
▶ RAF & USAAF: Operation Tonga: At 3:30hrs the third stage of the initial operation is completed when sixty-eight Horsas and four Hamilcar gliders towed

The mass of gliders used for Overlord is well illustrated here in this shot of British Airspeed Horsas to the right and centre and USAAF Waco Hadrians on the left (©R.J. Caruana Archives)

by Halifax and Albemarle aircraft deliver the 6th Airborne Division HQ troops and the 4th Anti-Tank Battery.

▶ RAF & USAAF: Operation Mallard: The final phase of the airborne assault commences at 1840hrs when the remainder of the 6th Airborne Division takes off from seven airfields. The operation is a great success with 246 of the 256 gliders that took off landing on their designated landing zones.

▶ RAF & USAAF: Operation Rob Roy: The first resupply mission is flown by fifty Dakotas during the evening.

7th June

▶ D-Day: The Allied forces break out of the beaches and move inland. The historic town of Bayeux is liberated; the famous Bayeux Tapestry had been safely stored near Le Mans since the war started. The other objectives for this first day, Carentan, St. Lô and Caen, are not liberated.

▶ RAF: Operation Cooney: Nine Albemarles drop fifty-six SAS troops in parties of three in a line across Brittany. Their task is to cut railway lines in eighteen pre-designated points to cut off Brest and western Brittany from the rest of France.

▶ RAF: HQs Nos.1304 and 1305 Wings, RAF Regiment with five Light Anti-Aircraft Squadrons go ashore at Juno Beach, Normandy.

▶ RAF: Nos.3207 and 3209 RAF Servicing Commando Units go ashore at Normandy to prepare emergency landing strips and advanced airfields.

▶ RAF: No.6225 Bomb Disposal Flight, RAF, is lost en route to Normandy when their landing craft is attacked and sunk. No.6225 (BD) Flight replace them on the 9th June.

8th June

▶ RAF: The first 12,000lb Tallboy bombs are dropped by No.617 Squadron on a railway tunnel near Saumur on the River Loire. One bomb scores a direct hit, blocking the tunnel for months.

▶ RAF: A Liberator of No.224 Squadron patrolling the Channel for U Boats, sinks two (U-629 and U-413) within twenty-two minutes of each other.

▶ RAF: Four Auster Mk IVs of No.652 Squadron are the first RAF aircraft to officially land in France at 08:15hrs. The Squadron conducts seven artillery shoot sorties by the end of the day.

9th June

▶ D-Day: American Generals realise that the objective of capturing Cherbourg by this date is impossible, so the decision is taken to cut off the entire Cotentin Peninsula.

▶ RAF: HQ No.83 Group is established in an orchard in Creully to supervise the construction and defence of airfields,

RAF Servicing Commandos refuel a Spitfire on an advanced landing ground in Normandy just after the invasion (©Air Ministry)

liaise with 21st Army Group and provide and control close air support operations over Normandy.

10th June

▶ RAF: Typhoons of No.124 Wing carry out rocket attacks on the HQ of the Panzer Group West at Château-la-Caine, followed by Mitchells bombing from 12,000ft. The Chief of Staff and many senior officers are killed and the HQ is put out of action until the 28th June.

▶ RAF: The first airfield in the Normandy beachhead, B.3 at St. Croix-sur-Mer built by the RAF Airfield Construction Wings, receives twelve Spitfires from No.222 Squadron.

12th June

▶ D-Day: All the beaches, except Utah, are linked.

▶ RAF: Sisters Mollie Giles and Iris 'Fluff' Ogilvie of the PMRAFNS (Princess Mary's Royal Air Force Nursing Service) are the first women to arrive in Normandy when they arrive with No.50 Mobile Field Hospital.

▶ RAF: Sixty-eight Light Anti-Aircraft Squadrons of the RAF Regiment are used to reinforce Army anti-aircraft units along the gun belt on the south–east coast of England designed to deal with the V1 flying bomb.

▶ RAF: Bomber Command starts a new offensive against German oil production when 303 aircraft attack the synthetic oil plant at Gelsenkirchen.

13th June

▶ Axis: The first Fieseler Fi 103 '*Vergeltungswaffe* 1' (V1) flying bomb launched against the UK falls at Swanscombe at 04:18hrs. By the end of WWII 8,892 V1s will be launched at the UK from ramps with a further 1,600 air-launched from He 111 bombers.

▶ RAF: The first three WAAF nursing

One of the first RAF Regiment Light Anti-Aircraft units in Normandy (©Air Ministry)

orderlies fly on operational duty in a Dakota of No.223 Squadron during the first air evacuation of casualties from Normandy.

14th June
▶ RAF: Wg Cdr J.E.Johnson of No.144 Wing is operating three Spitfire squadrons from B.3 at St. Croix-sur-Mer.
▶ RAF: The first V1 to be shot down by an aircraft falls to a Mosquito FB Mk VI flown by F/O J.F. Musgrove of No.605 Squadron.

16th June
▶ RAF: Bomber Command starts an intensive period of attacks against the flying bomb and rocket ('Noball') sites. This continues to 6th September.

19th June
▶ D-Day: Both Mulberry harbours on the Normandy coast are severely damaged by storms, the American one at Omaha beach is never repaired, but the British one at Arromanches (later known as 'Port Winston') is repaired and goes on to be used for 10 months, allowing 2.5 million men, half a million vehicles and 4 million tons of supplies to be brought ashore.

22nd June
▶ Allied: The Russians launch Operation Bagration, which clears German forces from Belarus and in so doing destroys German Army Group Centre.

23rd June
▶ RAF: A Spitfire F Mk XIV flown by F/O K.R. Collier of No.91 Squadron destroys a V1 by using the wing tip to topple the flying bomb. This is the first recorded incident of this method being used

25th June
▶ Finnish and Soviet forces clash in the Battle of Tali-Ihantala in which the Finns defeat the Russians, thus retaining their independence.
▶ US Army: Cherbourg is subject to a

Mulberry Harbour A at Omaha beach wrecked after the storms of the 19th June 1944. It was never repaired (©British Official)

naval bombardment by US and British ships in support of the US ground forces offensive on the port.

26th June
▶ US Army: American troops enter Cherbourg, but the Germans have destroyed the port facilities and it is not until September that it will become operational once more.
▶ RAF: Eight temporary airfields constructed by the RAF are operational in the Normandy bridgehead.

July
1944

▶ Luftwaffe: The new shades RLM 81 Olivbraun and 82 Hellgrün became standard colours during this month.

3rd July
▶ Allied: Soviet troops liberate Minsk.

9th July
▶ Allied: British and Canadian forces capture Caen.

12th July
▶ RAF: The RAF's first operational jet aircraft, the Gloster Meteor, enters service with No.616 Squadron at RAF Manston.

13th July
▶ Axis: Stalag Luft VI at Heydekrug, East Prussia is evacuated with prisoners transferred to other camps further west.
▶ Allied: The capital of Lithuania, Vilnius, is occupied by Soviet forces.

16th July
▶ Italy: The first contingent of the Brazilian Expeditionary Force arrives in Italy to fight alongside the Allied forces.

18th July
▶ RAF: The 2nd Army begins the breakout from the Normandy beachhead with No.83 Group flying 1,298 sorties and dropping 140 tons of bombs and using 70 tons of rockets in support of this. Visual Control Point (VCP) using an RAF controller in a tank with VHF radio directs the attacks for the first time.
▶ US Army: American troops liberate the city of Saint-Lô.
▶ RAF: British forces launch Operation Goodwood (18th–20th July), taking the Bourguébus Ridge, plus the area between Bretteville-sur-Laize and Vimont. The RAF commits 942 aircraft and drops 5,000 tons of bombs on five fortified villages to the east of Caen, with Mosquitos of No.8 (PFF) Group marking the targets.
▶ Allied: Canadian forces launch Operation Atlantic (18th–20th July) intended to capture Vaucelles, Colombelles, and the opposite banks of the Orne River.
▶ RAF: The RAF Test Pilots School is renamed the Empire Test Pilots School.

20th July
▶ Axis: Adolf Hitler survives an assassination attempt led by Claus von Stauffenberg.

23rd July
▶ RAF: Bomber Command mounts the first major raid on German cities for two months, when 629 aircraft attack Kiel.

25th July
▶ Allied: Operation Spring, also known as the Battle of Verrieres Ridge, is launched by Canadian forces. This three-phase operation lasts from the 25th to the 27th July and despite several German counter-attacks and high losses (450 killed and 1,100 wounded) the securing of the ridge is considered a strategic victory.
▶ Allied: The Battle of Tannenberg Line (25th July to 10th August 1944) is fought between German Army Detachment Narwa and the Soviet Leningrad Front for the strategically important Narva Isthmus.
▶ RAF: Operation Wildhorn III: A Dakota of No.267 Squadron takes off from Foggia, Italy and lands in a field 200 miles south of Warsaw to collect parts of a crashed V2 rocket that has been acquired by Polish partisans.

The Dakotas of No.267 Sqn at Foggia, which were used during Operation Wildhorn III
(©Royal Air Force/Air Ministry)

26th July
▶ Luftwaffe: Many accounts claim that the Messerschmitt Me 262 becomes the first jet fighter aircraft to score an operational victory on this date with Lt Alfred Schreiber in W/Nr.130017 claiming a de Havilland Mosquito from No.540 Squadron. However subsequent research shows that the aircraft, flown by Flt Lt Wall with his navigator F/O Lobban, evaded the Me 262 in a twenty-minute dogfight, however his aircraft was sufficiently damaged that he headed for Italy, not back to his base at Benson, and he made a successful emergency landing at the new base at Ferno, so the claim is only really a 'damaged'.

27th July
▶ RAF: A Meteor F Mk I of No.616 Squadron undertakes the first Allied (and RAF) jet operation, when it makes an anti-Diver (V1) patrol from Ashford to Robertsbridge in Kent.

28 July
▶ Luftwaffe: The first operational sortie of the Messerschmitt Me 163B-1a Komet, when aircraft from I./JG 400 at Brandis attack, without confirmed kills, two USAAF B-17 Flying Fortresses.

August
1944

3rd August
▶ RAF: Bomber Command sends 1,114 bombers against V1 launch sites in the Pas de Calais region, attacking three sites at Bois de Cassan, Forêt de Nieppe and Trossy-St-Maxim.

4th August
▶ RAF: The first successful Allied interception by a jet when a Meteor flown by W/O D. 'Dixie' Dean of No.616 Squadron uses the wing of his aircraft to tip over a V1.

8th August
▶ RAF: (The Warsaw Uprising) The RAF Chiefs of Staff request AM Sir John Slessor, Air Commander-in-Chief Mediterranean Allied Air Forces and Commander-in-Chief RAF Mediterranean and Middle East to comply with Polish requests for assistance if possible. Between the 8th August and 10th September thirty-one aircraft and 248 crew are lost mainly due to bad weather and Soviet refusals to allow the use of Russian-controlled forward airfields.

10th August
▶ RAF & USAAF: The white/black stripes applied prior to D-Day start to be removed from the upper fuselage and around the wings of most Allied aircraft between now and the 10th October 1944 (see also 10th September 1944).

12th August
▶ Allied: Allied forces liberate Florence, Italy.
▶ Allied: The world's first undersea oil pipeline (Operation Pluto – Pipeline Under The Ocean) is laid between Shanklin Chine on the Isle of Wight, England and Cherbourg in France.

15th August
▶ Luftwaffe: Directive issued deleting the colours RLM 65, 70, 71 and 74 and introducing the new colour RLM 83. RLM 70 is still retained for propellers, though.
▶ Allied: Operation Dragoon sees Allied forces landing in Southern France, with parachutists of the 1st Airborne Task Force going in first, followed by an amphibious assault by elements of the US 7th Army and on the following day by a force made up mainly of the French First Army. The landing is a success, causing the German Army Group G to abandon southern France.

16th August
▶ Luftwaffe: First flight of the Junkers Ju 287 V1 (pilot: Siegfried Holzbaur).

17th August
▶ RAF: This yellow leading edge wing markings applied to all Fighter Command aircraft is to be removed from all squadrons involved in ADGB (Air Defence of Great Britain) – anti-Diver (V1) operations from this date

19th August
▶ Allied: British, Canadian and Polish troops link up with American forces at Chambois, closing the Falaise Pocket.

20th August
▶ Allied: Argentan in the 'Falaise Pocket' liberated

P-47 Republic P-47D-28-RE Thunderbolt 44-19566 belongs to the 78th Fighter Group of the 8th Air Force, based at Duxford, and easily distinguishable from the black/white checks on the engine cowling. This machine has the partial stripes on the fuselage as per the official directive of the 10th August 1944 (©USAF)

21st August
▶ Allied: The 'Falaise Pocket' was sealed after a couple of German counter-attacks, trapping approximately 50,000 German soldiers inside. Although some managed to survive the continual Allied aerial bombardment, the losses were huge with Gen. Eisenhower stating that the battlefield of Falaise was unquestionably the greatest 'killing field' of any of the war areas, and that the scenes he encountered on inspecting the area 48 hours after closing the gap "could only be described by Dante".

24th August
▶ Allied: Allied forces liberate Paris, successfully bringing to a close Operation Overlord: Allied losses for the operation were 36,976 killed and 19,221 missing for the ground forces, while the air force losses were 16,714 killed or missing.

25th August
▶ Axis: In defiance of Hitler's orders to burn the city to the ground, General Dietrich von Choltitz surrenders Paris to the Allies.
▶ Allied: The Red Ball Express convoy system, using routes that are closed to civilian traffic, begins operations supplying materiel to Allied forces in France. At its peak, the Express carries 12,500 tons of supplies a day.

29th August
▶ The Slovak National Uprising (or 1944 Uprising) by Slovak resistance begins in an attempt to drive Axis forces from their nation and to overthrow the pro-Nazi government of Jozef Tiso. The fighting continued until the Soviet, Czech and Romanian armies liberated Slovakia in 1945.

September
1944

▶ Luftwaffe: At some point in this month a Factory Camouflage Directive is issued (or a related document, as neither survive) that specifies the use of the RLM 75 *Grauviolett* and 83 *Dunkelgrün* for the upper surfaces on the Fw 190D-9.

3rd September
▶ Allied: Allied forces liberate Brussels.

4th September
▶ Allied: 11th Armoured Division of the British Army liberates Antwerp.

5th September
▶ Allied: The Soviet Union declares war on Bulgaria.

6th September
▶ Allied: The Tartu Offensive in Estonia concludes with Soviet forces capturing the city.

8th September
▶ Axis: The first V2 rocket attack on London takes place.

10th September
▶ RAF & USAAF: Official instruction issued for the removal of the white/black stripes applied prior to D-Day from the upper fuselage and around the wings of all Allied aircraft (this actually started to be done from the 25th August).

12th September
▶ Allied: Allied forces from the north of France (Operation Overlord) and those from the South (Operation Dragoon) link up near Dijon.

14th September
▶ Allied: The Riga Offensive is launched by the 1st, 2nd and 3rd Baltic Fronts of the Soviet army in Estonia. This leads to Hitler ordering the evacuation of all German troops from Estonia.

17th September
▶ Allied: Operation Market Garden, the Allied airborne landings in the Netherlands and Germany, begin.
▶ Allied: Soviets launch the Tallinn Offensive from the Emajõgi River Front, in the hope of cutting off the retreating German Army Detachment Narwa in Estonia.

19th September
▶ Allied: The Battle of Hürtgen Forest begins, this is the biggest battle on German soil to be fought during WWII, it will cost the lives of 33,000 Americans and 28,000 Germans and lasts until the 16th December.

22nd September
▶ Allied: Soviet forces reach Tallinn, Estonia and call a halt to their offensive, although the Prime Minister in Duties of the President of Estonia Jüri Uluots and 80,000 Estonian civilians manage to escape to Sweden.

24th September
▶ Allied: The US 45th Infantry Division takes Épinal, the capital of the Vosges Department, before crossing the Moselle River and entering the western foothills of the Vosges mountain range.

26th September
▶ Allied: Allied troops withdraw after the failure of Operation Market Garden, the operation resulted in 15,326 to 17,200 casualties along with the loss of 144 transport aircraft.

October
1944

▶ Luftwaffe: The first operation use of the Fw 190D-9 by III./JG54 takes place early in this month.
▶ Luftwaffe: Messerschmitt issue *Oberflächebschutzliste* 8 Os 109K designating RLM 74/75/76 as the camouflage colours for the Bf 109K series.

The Typhoon won its laurels as a potent ground attack aircraft armed with its four 20mm cannon and up to eight rocket projectiles. This picture was taken at a captured airfield in France soon after D-Day. Note how the previous unequal black/white wing bands have now been substituted with the equal 18in. 'invasion' stripes of the same colours
(©R.J. Caruana Archives)

5th October
▶ RAF: The first Me 262 to be actually shot down, not forced into the ground as had been the case on two separate occasions in August and October 1944, is jointly claimed by Sqn Ldr Smith, Flt Lt Davenport, Flt Lt Everard, F/O Mackay and F/O Sinclair of No.401 Squadron, Royal Canadian Air Force near Nijmegen in the Netherlands. The aircraft, W/Nr.170093 was flown by *Hptm.* Hans C. Buttmann of 3./KG51.

6th October
▶ Allied: The Battle of Debrecen (or the Debrecen Offensive Operation) starts on the Eastern Front with Marsahl Rodion Malinovsky's 2nd Ukrainian Front having Debrecen, Hungary as their objective.

13th October
▶ Allied: Latvia's capital, Riga, is taken by the Soviet Army.
▶ Axis: The first V2 rocket falls on Antwerp.

14th October
▶ Axis: Field Marshal Erwin Rommel commits suicide rather than face execution.

14th–18th October
▶ USAAF & RAF: Due to the 'Transportation Plan' of strategic bombing, rail shipments of coal from the Ruhr cease completely during this period.

18th October
▶ Axis: The *Volkssturm* ('People's Storm') militia is officially announced, this being set up by the Nazi Party on Adolf Hitler's orders, not as part of the German Army.

20th October
▶ Allied: Yugoslav Partisans and the Soviet Army liberate Belgrade.

21st October
▶ Allied: The first German city to fall to the Allies, Aachen, is captured by American troops.

25th October
▶ Allied: Kirkenes is liberated by the Soviet Army, the first town in Norway to be so.

November
1944

▶ Luftwaffe: The first production Ta 152C flies during this month.
▶ Luftwaffe: Focke-Wulf issue Ober-

flächebschutzliste 8 Os 152 designating RLM 81/82/76 as the camouflage colours for the 'Ta 152' series (the document does not clarify if this meant the C or H series, or both – The H-series certainly used RLM 81/82/76, whilst the C-series seems to have initially been in the D-series scheme of RLM 75/83).

▶ Luftwaffe: The last version of the Heinkel He 219, the A-7 series, goes into production during this month.

12th November
▶ RAF: The German battleship Tirpitz is attacked by Lancaster from Nos.9 and 617 Squadrons during Operation Catechism. Of the twenty-nine Tallboy 12,000lb bombs dropped, two hit the ship and one is a near miss causing sufficient damage to cause the already damaged ship to list to port; this increases from 15° to 60° and at 09:50am, just 15 minutes after the attack, the battleship rapidly rolls (the wreck remains after the war and was scrapped in an operation lasting from 1948 to 1957).

16th November
▶ Allied: The First and Ninth US Armies begin Operation Queen against the Ruhr River as a staging point for the move across the river to the Rhine. This operation begins with one of the heaviest Allied tactical bombing raids of the war.

24th November
▶ Axis: German troops evacuate the West Estonian Archipelago in the Baltic Sea.

26th November
▶ Luftwaffe: Dornier issue *Oberflächebschutzliste* 8 Os 335A designating RLM 81/82/76 as the camouflage colours for the Do 335A series; oddly the instruction lists both 81 and 82 shades as '*Dunkelgrün*'?

The British Mulberry harbour off Arromanches, Normandy seen in September 1944, having been repaired after the storms of the 19th June (©British Official)

December
1944

12th & 13th December
▶ Italy: British troops fail in their attempt to take the hilltop town of Borgo Tossignano.

15th December
▶ Allied: American band leader Glenn Miller disappears in heavy fog over the English Channel while flying in a UC-64 Norseman from RAF Twinwoods Farm, Clapham to Paris; Lt. Col. Norman Baessell and the pilot, John Morgan, are also killed.

16th December
▶ Axis: German forces begin the Ardennes offensive, later called the 'Battle of the Bulge'.
▶ Luftwaffe: During the period of the Battle of the Bulge (16th to 31st December) the Luftwaffe lose 400 pilots, either killed or missing in support of the operation.

20th December
▶ Allied: The United States Women Air Force Service Pilots (WASPs) are disbanded.

24th December
▶ Axis: German armour reaches the furthest point during the Battle of the Bulge at Celles.
▶ Luftwaffe: V1 flying bombs launched from Heinkel He 111s flying over the North Sea are aimed at Manchester, with at least 27 being killed and more than 100 injured in the Oldham area.

26th December
▶ Allied: American troops repulse German forces at Bastogne.

January
1945

▶ Luftwaffe: During the early part of 1945 you see the move from the standard RLM 75/83 upper surface camouflage to the new RLM 81/82 combination.
▶ Luftwaffe: Series-production of the Dornier Do 335 starts during this month
▶ Luftwaffe: The first Heinkel He 162 test unit '*Erprobungskommando* 162' is set up this month at Rechlin.

Macchi C.205V. C.205Vs, still wearing Luftwaffe markings, are here seen at Lonate Pozzolo before being handed over to the 1° Gruppo of the ANR (R.J. Caruana Archives)

1st January
▶ Luftwaffe: *Operation Bodenplatte* (Baseplate) is launched, having been delayed by bad weather from its original date of the 16th December 1944, by the Luftwaffe in an attempt to cripple Allied air forces in the Low Countries. Over 800 fighter-bombers make a low-level surprise attack on Allied airfields in Belgium and the Netherlands. Surprise is complete and 224 aircraft are destroyed, of which 144 are from the RAF, while a further 84 are damaged beyond repair. The losses will be made good in two weeks though, but the Luftwaffe lose 300 aircraft, 143 pilots killed, 70 captured and 21 wounded, and not all to Allied airfield defences, as many are lost to their own Anti-Aircraft because these units had not been forewarned of the attack.

3rd January
▶ RAF: 2nd TAF issue orders that all aircraft attached to the Command are to have their spinners painted black or camouflaged instead of Sky or the individual Squadron or Flight colours, and the Sky rear fuselage band is also to be deleted.

7th January
▶ RAF: The RAF revert to red, white and blue (Type C) roundels on the upper surfaces of all aircraft except those involved in night flying and those in the South–East Asia and Pacific theatres.

16th January
▶ Axis: Adolf Hitler takes up residence in the *Führerbunker* in Berlin.

17th January
▶ Allied: Soviet forces occupy Warsaw, Poland.

Wrecked Typhoon on Eindhoven airfield (©British Official)

silver (RLM 01) or red oxide.

19th January
▶ Axis: Stalag Luft VII at Bankau is evacuated with Allied POWs starting a walk to the west that was to become known as 'The Long March'.

20th January
▶ RAF: Gloster Meteor F Mk Is of No.616 Squadron are deployed to Europe for the first time, being based at Melsbroek, Belgium. They are painted overall white initially, to identify them to Allied pilots who had never seen the type before.

23rd January
▶ Axis: Hungary agrees to an armistice with the Allies.
▶ Axis: Operation Hannibal, the evacuation by sea of German troops and civilians from the Courland Pocket, East Prussia and the Polish Corridor, is ordered by German Grand Admiral Karl Dönitz.

One of No.144 Squadron's Beaufighters that crash-landed on return to RAF Dallachy after 'Black Friday' on the 9th February 1945 (©British Official)

18th January
▶ Luftwaffe: Heinkel issue *Oberflächeb-schutzliste* 8 Os 162A designating RLM 81/82 as the upper camouflage colours for the He 162A series, the undersides being usually left unpainted. Note that there are photos proving that many of these machines used older colours, with the combinations of 70/81 and 71/82 being known. The wooden elements (wings, tail, u/c doors etc.) were usually primed in grey, grey-green (RLM 02),

27th January
▶ Allied: The Soviet Army liberates Auschwitz and Birkenau concentration camps.
▶ Axis: POWs at Stalag Luft III are given one hour to gather their belongings and evacuate the camp, thus joining thousands of others in 'The Long March'.

30th January
▶ Axis: Adolf Hitler makes his last public speech to be delivered personally, via a radio broadcast.

February
1945

▶ Luftwaffe: The first Heinkel He 162s are delivered to I./JG1 at Parchim.

2nd February
▶ Luftwaffe: The first flight of the Horten Ho.IX V2 (powered by Jumo 004 engines) is made at Oranienburg.

8th February
▶ Allied: Fighter-bombers of the 2nd Tactical Air Force (2 TAF) undertake extensive armed reconnaissance and attacks on enemy headquarters, bridges and trains in preparations for the Allied operations to cross the River Rhine.

9th February
▶ RAF: Thirty-two Bristol Beaufighter from the Dallachy Wing, escorted by ten P-51 Mustangs of No.65 Squadron, make an unsuccessful attack on the German destroyer Z33 and its escorting vessels sheltering in Førde Fjord, Norway. Nine Beaufighters and one Mustang are shot down by the intensive anti-aircraft fire and the Fw 190s, whilst many that do get back crash-land and are written off; this day becomes known as 'Black Friday'.

13th February
▶ Allied: Soviet forces liberate Budapest, Hungary.
▶ Allied: The first of four raids by the Royal Air Force and USAAF on the city of Dresden, Germany. 805 RAF and 527 USAAF bombers drop 3,900 tons of high explosive and incendiary bombs. The resulting firestorm destroys 1,600 acres and kills 22,700-25,000 people.

15th February
▶ Luftwaffe: The second test flight of the Horten Ho.IX V2 is made.

16th February
▶ Allied: Venezuela declares war on Germany.

20th February
▶ Luftwaffe: B.Br.Nr.2/45 g.Kdos is

issued designating the application of recognition bands on the rear fuselage of all Luftwaffe aircraft involved in the Defence of the Reich (RVD). Such bands have been applied since mid-1944, but this is the first official document specifying the colours per unit: JG1 (bright red), JG2 (yellow/white/yellow), JG3 (white), JG4 (black/white/black), JG5 (black-yellow), JG6 (bright red/white/bright red), JG7 (blue/red), JG11 (yellow), JG26 (black/white), JG27 (bright green), JG51 (bright green/white/bright green), JG52 (red/white), JG53 (black), JG54 (bright green), JG77 (white/green), JG300 (bright blue/white/bright blue), JG301 (yellow/red).

▶ RAF: The first of thirty-six consecutive nights that Mosquitos of the Light Night Striking Force (LNSF) attack Berlin, the last raid being the night of the 27th/28th March.

21st February
▶ Axis: The last V2-rocket is successfully launched from Peenemünde.

22nd February
▶ RAF: Operation Clarion: Heavy and medium RAF bombers undertake raids on rail bridges and viaducts, road and rail traffic and marshalling and repair yards along a line from Bremen to Koblenz in preparation for the crossing of the River Rhine; over 9,000 Allied aircraft are involved.
▶ Italy: End of the Battle of Monte Castello.

23rd February
▶ Luftwaffe: Messerschmitt issue *Oberflächebschutzliste* 8 Os 262A designating RLM 81/82/76 as the camouflage colours for the Me 262A series.
▶ Allied: The German garrison in Poznan capitulates to Russian and Polish troops.
▶ RAF: Largest bombing raid on Pforzheim is carried out by the Royal Air Force, resulting in 17,600 deaths.
▶ Allied: Turkey joins the war on the Allied side.

March
1945

2nd March
▶ Axis: The Bachem Ba 349 Natter is test launched at Stetten am kalten Markt. The canopy comes loose just after launch and the pilot, Lothar Sieber, is killed.
▶ USAAF & Luftwaffe: The Me 262A is first encountered by USAAF 8th AF bomber crews when a raid on the synthetic oil refineries at Leipzig is intercepted by the jets near Dresden.

3rd March
▶ RAF: Royal Air Force bombs accidentally fall on the Bezuidenhout neighbourhood in The Hague, killing 511 people.
▶ Luftwaffe: Me 262s of Jagdgeschwader 7 Nowotny attack 8th Air Force bomber formations over Dresden, en route to oil targets at Essen, shooting down three bombers.

5th March
▶ Italy: Brazilian troops liberate Castelnuovo (Vergato), in the last Allied operations in Italy before the Spring Offensive.

7th March
▶ Allied: At the end of Operation Lumberjack, American troops seize the Ludendorff Bridge over the Rhine at Remagen in Germany and begin to cross; in the next 10 days 25,000 troops with equipment are able to cross.

8th March
▶ Allied: Operation Sunrise: Waffen-SS *General* Karl Wolff meets with Allen Welsh Dulles of the United States Office of Strategic Services at Lucerne in neutral Switzerland to negotiate surrender of the Axis forces in Italy to the Allies.

12th March
▶ RAF: 1,108 bombers attack Dortmund, making it the largest number of RAF aircraft to attack a single target in WWII, with 4,851 tons of bombs dropped (another record for a single raid).
▶ USAAF: Swinemünde is destroyed by the USAAF killing an estimated 8,000 to 23,000 civilians, mostly refugees saved by Operation Hannibal.
▶ Luftwaffe: The Gotha Go 229 (Horten Ho.IX) is included in the *Jäger-Notprogramm* (Emergency Fighter Programme) for accelerated production.

14th March
▶ Luftwaffe: *Jagdverband* 44 (JV 44) takes delivery of its first Me 262s

18th March
▶ USAAF: 1,250 USAAF bombers attack Berlin.

19th March
▶ Axis: Adolf Hitler orders that all industries, military installations, machine shops, transportation and communications facilities in Germany be destroyed.

21st March
▶ RAF: Seventeen Mosquitos of Nos.21, 464 and 467 Squadrons, escorted by Mustangs of No.64 Squadron, destroy the main buildings of the Gestapo HQ in

Group Captain J.E. Fauquier, the Commanding Officier of No.617 Squadron, poses alongside a 22,000lb 'Grand Slam' underneath a Lancaster (©British Official)

the Shellhaus building in Copenhagen. One Mosquito crashes on a nearby school, with much loss of life, AVM B. Embry (AOC 2nd TAF) flies as 'Wg Cdr Smith' during this operation.
▶ RAF: Seventy-two Kittyhawks and Mustangs of No.239 Wing bomb shipping and storage areas in Venice harbour, the only bombing attack made against the historic city in WWII.

24th March
▶ Allied: Operation Varsity: In support of the amphibious assault across the River Rhine tug aircraft of Nos.38 and 46 Groups tow 439 gliders to drop zones near Wesel. Nos.3 and 5 Parachute Brigades are dropped from aircraft of the US No.IX Troop Carrier Command. 2nd TAF supply close-support fire and the whole area is subject to fighter-bomber and bomber attacks on the rail and road communications for a few days prior to the assault.

29th March
▶ Axis: The last V1 to be shot down over the UK falls near Sittingbourne. Of the 3,957 V1s destroyed, 1,847 were by aircraft, 1,866 by anti-aircraft fire, 232 by balloons and 12 by guns of the Royal Navy. The highest scoring RAF pilot was Sqn Ldr J. Berry of No.501 Squadron with fifty-nine and one shared.

31st March
▶ Allied: The British Commonwealth Air Training Plan, also known as the Empire Training Scheme prior to June 1942, is officially ended.

Late March
▶ Luftwaffe: Jagdverband 44 (JV 44) has its first aerial victory, when Oberst Steinhoff claims an Ilyushin Il-2.

April

1945

3rd April
▶ Allied: Operation Exodus: The repatriation of liberated POWs from Germany begins.

4th April
▶ Allied: American troops liberate their first Nazi concentration camp, Ohrdruf in Germany.

6th April
▶ Allied: Sarajevo is liberated from Nazi Germany and the Independent State of Croatia (a fascist puppet state) by Yugoslav Partisans.

7th April
▶ RAF: Operation Amherst: Forty-six Stirlings of No.38 Group drop French paratroops of the 2nd and 3rd Regiments de Chasseurs Parachutistes on twenty selected drop zones in northern Holland

The last pilots from the British Commonwealth Air Training Plan take the salute to mark the end of the plan on the 31st March 1945 (©Air Ministry)

in support of the First Canadian Army's operation to secure airfields and road and rail bridges. Despite bad weather all are safely dropped 'blind' thanks to the use of the Gee navigation aid.
▶ Luftwaffe: The only operational flight of the Luftwaffe ramming unit known as the *Sonderkommando Elbe* takes place, resulting in the loss of some 24 B-17s and B-24s of the USAAF 8th Air Force.

8th April
▶ Luftwaffe: II./JG 1 at Marienehe start to convert from the Fw 190 to the He 162; they never become operational, as all staff and pilots are used to fill spaces in other units, and it officially disbands on the 24th April.

9th April
▶ RAF: A force of Lancasters attack Keil resulting in Admiral Scheer being hit and capsizing, Admiral Hipper being seriously damaged and scuttled and the cruiser Emden badly damaged.
▶ RAF: Mosquitos of the Banff Wing mount a daylight strike in the Kattegat, sinking U-boats U-804 and U-1065 with rockets.

11th April
▶ Allied: Buchenwald concentration camp is liberated by the US Army.

14th April
▶ Allied: The First Canadian Army assumes military control of the Netherlands.

15th April
▶ Allied: Bergen-Belsen concentration camp is liberated by British and Canadian troops.
▶ Allied: The Canadian First Army reaches the coast of the northern Netherlands and captures Arnhem.

16th April
▶ The Battle of Berlin begins.
▶ RAF: Sixteen Lancasters of No.617 Squadron drop 12,000lb Tallboy bombs to sink the German pocket battleship Lutzow at Swinemunde.

17th April
▶ Italy: Brazilian forces liberate Montese, Italy.
▶ Axis: The Wieringermeer in the Netherlands is flooded by occupying German forces.

19th April
▶ RAF & USAAF: The Combined Chiefs of Staff issue a directive that stipulates all further operations by strategic air forces should be diverted to support the ground forces, to come into effect on the 5th May.
▶ Luftwaffe: The He 162 has its first operational success, when it shoots down an RAF Hawker Tempest.

20th April
▶ Axis: On his 56th birthday Adolf Hitler leaves the *Führerbunker* for the last time to decorate a group of Hitler Youth soldiers in Berlin.

22nd April
▶ Luftwaffe: US Army forces capture the Dornier plant at Oberpfaffenhofen and find eleven Do 335A-1 and two Do 335A-12 airframes plus many more partially built ones.
▶ Axis: An offer of German surrender to the Western Allies, excluding Russia, is made by Heinrich Himmler via Count Bernadotte.

23rd April
▶ Axis: Field Marshall Hermann Göring sends a telegram to Hitler seeking confirmation that he should take over leadership of Germany in accordance with the decree of 29th June 1941, but Hitler regards this as treason.

24th April
▶ RAF: Gloster Meteor F Mk Is of No.616 Squadron carry out ground-attack sorties against Nordholz, the first operational use of the jet over Continental Europe.

25th April
▶ RAF: Hitler's 'Eagle's Nest' chalet and the SS barracks at Berchtesgaden are attacked by 359 Lancasters and 16 Mosquitos.
▶ RAF: Fourteen Lancasters carry out the last mine laying operation of WWII in Oslo Fjord
▶ RAF: Operation Exodus: The number of POWs needing to be repatriated from Germany is such that SHAEF (Supreme Headquarters Allied Expeditionary Force) asks Bomber Command for its assistance.
▶ Allied: American and Soviet troops link up at the Elbe River, cutting Germany in two.
▶ USAAF: The last full-scale operation by the USAAF 8th AF of the European War when B-17s attack the Skoda armaments factory at Pilsen in Czechoslovakia and B-24s bomb the rail complexes surrounding Hitler's mountain retreat at Berchtesgaden.

25th–26th April
▶ RAF: The last major strategic heavy bombing raid by RAF Bomber Command is undertaken by 107 Lancasters to destroy the oil refinery at Tønsberg in southern Norway.

26th April
▶ Luftwaffe: *Jagdverband* 44 (JV 44) commander, General Adolf Galland is wounded in the knee and passes command of the unit to Heinz Bär.
▶ Axis: The Battle of Bautzen, the last German panzer-offensive in WWII, ends with the city being recaptured.
▶ Allied: The British 3rd Infantry Division captures Bremen.
▶ Allied: The surrender of Nazi forces means that the British and Canadians now control the German border with Switzerland from Basle to Lake Constance.

27th April
▶ Allied: The Western Allies reject any offer of surrender by Germany other than on unconditional terms on all fronts.

28th April
▶ Italy: Benito Mussolini and his mistress, Clara Petacci, are executed by Italian partisans as they attempt to flee the country. Their bodies are then hung by their heels outside a garage in the public square of Milan.
▶ Allied: The Canadian First Army captures Emden and Wilhelmshaven.

29th April
▶ RAF & USAAF: Operation Manna: The beginning of food dropping operations to the starving Dutch population begins with 250 RAF bombers. The operation continues to the 8th May by which time 3,159 sorties deliver 6,685 tons of food. The USAAF undertake 5,343 sorties and deliver 3,700 tons under Operation Chowhound.
▶ Italy: In the royal palace in Caserta, *Lieutenant-Colonel* Viktor von Schweinitz (representing *General* Heinrich von Vietinghoff) and *SS-Obersturmbannfuehrer* Eugen Wenner (representing *Waffen-SS General* Karl Wolf) sign an unconditional instrument of surrender for all Axis powers forces in Italy, taking effect on 2nd May. Italian General Rodolfo Graziani orders the *Esercito Nazionale Repubblicano* forces under his command to lay down their arms.
▶ Italy: Brazilian forces liberate the commune of Fornovo di Taro, Italy, from German troops.
▶ Axis: Adolf Hitler marries Eva Braun in a closed civil ceremony in the Führerbunker and signs his last will and testament.

30th April
▶ Axis: Adolf Hitler and his wife of one day, Eva Braun, commit suicide as the Red Army approaches the Führerbunker in Berlin. Karl Dönitz succeeds Hitler as President of Germany (Reichspräsident) and Joseph Goebbels succeeds as Chancellor of Germany (Reichskanzler), in accordance with Hitler's political testament of the previous day.

May
1945

1st May
▶ Axis: Hamburg Radio announces that Hitler has died in battle, "fighting up to his last breath against Bolshevism."
▶ Axis: Joseph Goebbels and his wife Magda commit suicide after killing their six children. Karl Dönitz appoints Lutz Graf Schwerin von Krosigk as the new Chancellor of Germany in the Flensburg Government.
▶ Luftwaffe: General Adolf Galland makes a request to General Eisenhower for a special surrender to be granted to Jagdverband 44 (JV 44). This request is flown to Schleißheim in a Fi 156 by *Maj.* W. Herget and *Capt.* H. Kessler and although an agreement is given by the Americans and Galland writes his reply,

Returning Allied POWs are seen on arrival back in the UK during Operation Exodus (©Air Ministry)

A Gloster Meteor F Mk I of No.616 Squadron seen in the all-white scheme applied to these machines when they deployed to Europe. This one is seen at Melsbroek, Belgium (©Air Ministry)

it never reaches the Allies because the Fi 156 was shot down over Schleißheim.
▶ Italy: Troops of the Yugoslav 4th Army, together with the Slovene 9th Corpus NOV, enter Trieste.

2nd May
▶ RAF: Bomber Command mounts its last raid again Germany when a force of 126 Mosquitos attack Kiel. Two Radio Counter Measures Halifax aircraft supporting the raid are lost, becoming the last Bomber Command losses of WWI (three crew members survive). Throughout WWII Bomber Command lost 55,000 crew in operations and accidents, with a further 18,700 wounded, injured or made POWs; the highest loss ratio of any of the British military commands during the war.
▶ RAF: Battle of Britain pilot Wg Cdr E.J.B. Nicholson VC is killed when the Liberator he is an observer on crashes in the Bay of Bengal en route to the target.
▶ Allied: The Soviet Union announces the fall of Berlin. Soviet soldiers hoist the Red flag over the Reich Chancellery.
▶ Allied: Prague occupied by Soviet forces.
▶ Allied: Lübeck is liberated by the British Army.
▶ Italy: The total surrender of Axis troops in Italy comes into effect.
▶ Italy: Troops of the New Zealand Army 2nd Division enter Trieste a day after the Yugoslavs and the German Army in Trieste surrenders to them.
▶ Axis: Following the death or resignation of the Hitler Cabinet in Germany, the Schwerin von Krosigk cabinet first meets.

3rd May
▶ Luftwaffe: All of JG 1's surviving He 162s are restructured into two groups, I. *Einsatz* ('Combat') and II. *Sammel* ('Collection').
▶ Axis: Rocket scientist Wernher von Braun and 120 members of his team surrender to American troops.

4th May
▶ RAF: Beaufighters of Nos.236 and 254 Squadrons sink four U-boats attempting to escape to Norway on the surface.
▶ RAF: Eleven RAF Regiment Light Anti-Aircraft, Rifle and Armoured Car Squadrons move ahead of the British Army to occupy Schleswig-Holstein up to the Danish border. In doing so they capture 50,000 German naval and air force personnel, including Hitler's successor, Grand Admiral Doenitz.
▶ Axis: German surrender at Lüneburg Heath: All German armed forces in northwest Germany, Denmark and the Netherlands surrender unconditionally to Field Marshal Bernard Montgomery, officially coming into effect on the 5th May at 08:00 hours British Double (and German) Summer Time.
▶ Allied: The Netherlands is liberated by British and Canadian troops.
▶ Allied: Denmark is liberated.
▶ Axis: Admiral Karl Dönitz orders all U-boats to cease offensive operations and return to their bases in Norway.

5th May
▶ RAF & USAAF: All operations by strategic air forces were now solely in support of the ground forces, as per the Combined Chiefs of Staff directive of the 19th April.
▶ Allied: The US 11th Armored Division liberates Mauthausen concentration camp and Canadian soldiers liberate the city of Amsterdam.

6th May
▶ Axis: Mildred Gillars ('Axis Sally') delivers her last propaganda broadcast to Allied troops.
▶ Allied: American troops liberate Ebensee concentration camp in Austria.

7th May
▶ Axis: General Alfred Jodl signs the unconditional German Instrument of Surrender at Reims, France, ending Germany's participation in the war, officially coming into effect on 8th May at 23:01 hours Central European Time (00:01 hours 9th May German Summer Time).
▶ RAF: The last U-Boat to be sunk by an aircraft of Coastal Command, U-320, is attacked by a Catalina of No.210 Squadron. Throughout WWII Coastal Command had sunk 207 U-Boats and 513,804 tons of Axis shipping for the loss of 5,866 aircrew and 1,777 aircraft.

8th May
▶ Allied: Victory in Europe Day (VE Day) as Nazi Germany surrenders, marking the end of WWII in Europe, with the final surrender being to the Soviets in Berlin, attended by representatives of the Western Powers.
▶ Allied: Canadian troops move into Amsterdam.
▶ Axis: Surrender of the Dodecanese is signed in Symi.
▶ RAF: Operation Doomsday: Aircraft of No.38 Group, RAF, transport 7,000 troops and 2,000 tons of equipment to Oslo, Stavanger and Kristiansands to establish Allied control in Norway. The operation takes five days due to poor weather.

A Lancaster is loaded with food bundles to be dropped over Holland as part of 'Operation Manna' (©Air Ministry)

- **Bristol Beaufighter TF Mk X, NE429, P6•S flown by P/O E.F.G. Burrowes (F/O D.A. Young navigator) of No.489 (RNZAF) Squadron, 30th July 1944**
  Dark Sea Grey upper surfaces; Sky undersides; black/white invasion stripes around rear fuselage and wings; Type C1 roundels on fuselage sides and Type B roundels above wings; codes in Medium Sea Grey, note previous codes painted over

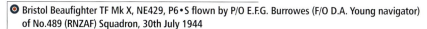

- **Mosquito FB Mk VI, LR347, •T flown by Flt Lt S. Nunn (DFC), No.235 Squadron, Portreath, June 1944**
  Extra Dark Sea Grey upper surfaces with Sky undersides; Night/white bands around wings and fuselage; dull red code 'T'; Night serial; red spinners; Type B type roundels above wings

- **North American Mustang Mk III, FB354, SZ•P, No.316 Squadron, Andrews, March 1945**
  Ocean Grey/Dark Green upper surfaces with Light Grey ANA 602 undersides; red/white nose stripes; Sky codes and rear fuselage band; Night serial. Polish flag on nose, unit badge below windscreen (with two kill markings aft); 'B' type roundels above wings

- **North American Mustang Mk IV (11180), KH653, QV•P, No.19 Squadron, Peterhead, March 1945**
  Olive Drab ANA 613/Sea Grey ANA 603 upper surfaces with Light Grey ANA 602 undersides; blue/white/red roundels above wings; Sky rear fuselage band and codes; Night serial; yellow/Night bands around nose; yellow wing leading edges

- **North American Mustang Mk Ia, FD472, •M, flown on D-Day by Flt Lt Tuele of No.268 Squadron, operating from Gatwick**
  Ocean Grey/Dark Green upper surfaces with Medium Sea Grey undersides; black/white 18in wide bands only below rear fuselage and wings; Sky spinner, code and rear fuselage band; Night serial; standard post-May 1942 national markings

- **Supermarine Spitfire Mk IXc, MK392, JE•J, flown by Wg Cdr 'Johnnie' Johnson, CO No.144 Wing, summer 1944**
  Ocean Grey/Dark Green upper surfaces with Medium Sea Grey undersides; Sky rear fuselage band and codes; Night serial; black/white bands around wings and fuselage; red Maple Leaf within a white disc below windscreen; white spinner

- **Supermarine Spitfire Mk XVI, TB900, 9N•F, 'Winston Churchill', No.127 Squadron, The Netherlands, April 1945**
  Ocean Grey/Dark Green upper surfaces with Medium Sea Grey undersides; Sky spinner, codes and rear fuselage band; name in white below windscreen

- **Supermarine Spitfire LF Mk IXc, MJ840, DU•L, No.312 (Czech) Squadron, 11th June 1944**
  Ocean Grey/Dark Green/Medium Sea Grey scheme with Sky spinner and codes; yellow leading edge to wings; black/white bands around wings and fuselage; Czech roundel under both sides of windscreen while unit badge is carried only on port side. Note fuselage bands roughly painted leaving an irregular boarder around codes and roundel; Type C1 roundel on fuselage, Type B above and Type C under wings

- **Supermarine Spitfire PR Mk XIX, RM640/F, No.682 Squadron, San Severo (Italy), summer 1944**
  PRU Blue overall with Type B roundels on fuselage sides and above wings; white code, light grey serial

- **Supermarine Spitfire PR Mk XIX, RM643/Z, No.541 Squadron, RAF Benson, 1944**
  PRU Blue overall with black/white bands around fuselage; Type B roundels on fuselage and above wings; serial and code in light grey

- **Hawker Tempest Mk V Series 2, JN862, JF•Z flown by Flt Lt Remy van Lierde, No.3 Squadron, August 1944**
  Ocean Grey/Dark Green upper surfaces with Medium Sea Grey undersides; Sky spinner, rear fuselage band and codes, the latter thinly outlined in red; Night serial, black/white 18in bands around rear fuselage and chordwise around the wings; thin black/yellow/red band around tip of spinner

- **Tempest Mk V, SN129, SA•M flown by Sqn Ldr Jimmy Sheddan, No.486 Squadron, April 1945**
  Ocean Grey/Dark Green upper surfaces; Medium Sea Grey undersides; five and a half victories marked in white (shown in black in scrap view for clarity) and rank pennant ahead of cockpit; Night spinner

- **Hawker Typhoon Mk Ib, MN293, TP•D, No.198 Squadron, RAF Thorney Island, June 1944**
  Ocean Grey/Dark Green/Medium Sea Grey scheme with Sky codes and rear fuselage band; red spinner with white backplate; black/white bands under wings and around fuselage; serial partially overpainted. Note 'D' of code repositioned on engine cowling

- **Hawker Typhoon Mk Ib, MN526, TP•V, No.198 Squadron, Plumetot (France), July 1944**
  Ocean Grey/Dark Green/Medium Sea Grey scheme with red spinner and 'TP' of code, Sky rear band and 'V' of code, 'V' repeated on fin in white; 18in (61cm) black and white bands under fuselage and wings; Type B roundels above wings

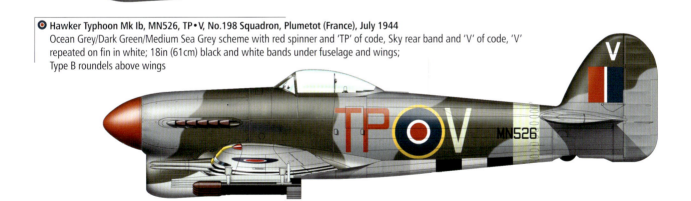

- **Hawker Typhoon Mk Ib, SW411, PR•J flown by Sqn Ldr L.W.F. Stark, CO No.609 Squadron, Plantlunne (B.103, Germany), May 1945**
  Ocean Grey and Dark Green upper surfaces with Medium Sea Grey undersides; Sky codes; Sky fuselage band painted over; black spinner with yellow backplate; unit badge and rank pennant below windscreen; red/white/blue roundels above and below wings. Note: inside of undercarriage doors were yellow, edged in white

- **Armstrong Withworth Albemarle Mk V, V1823, P5•S, No.297 Squadron, RAF Brize Norton, summer 1944**
  Dark Earth/Dark Green/Night scheme with black/white bands around wings and fuselage; codes and serials in dull red

- **Martin B-26C-45 Marauder, S/No.42-107657, Groupe de Bombardement I/22, operating within the 1st TAF, Italy, late 1944**
  Natural metal overall with black serials; roundels in six positions; unit badge on nose.
  Note three mission markings and only one side gun pack per side

- **Bristol Beaufort Mk II, ML569, PI•K, No.762 Naval Air Squadron, Halesworth, 1945**
  White overall with Extra Dark Sea Grey uppersurfaces of wings, tailplane and fuselage spine; codes in yellow, serials in black; Type C roundels above wings

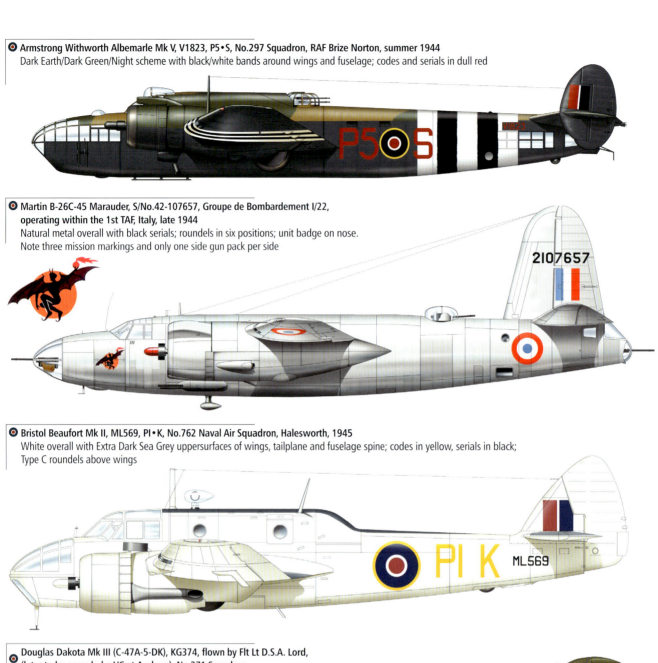

- **Douglas Dakota Mk III (C-47A-5-DK), KG374, flown by Flt Lt D.S.A. Lord, (later to be awarded a VC at Arnhem), No.271 Squadron**
  Olive Drab/Netural Grey scheme with black/white bands around wings and rear fuselage; code in Sky, serial in black

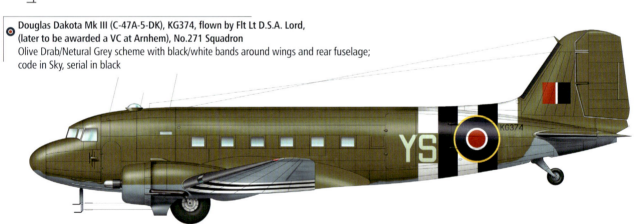

- **Handley-Page Halifax B Mk V Series IA, LL312, 9U•L, No.644 Squadron RAF, 1944**
  Dark Earth/Dark Green uppersurfaces; Night undersides; dull red codes and serial; black/white bands (handpainted) around rear fuselage; Type C1 roundels on fuselage sides, Type B roundels above wings

- **Douglas Boston Mk IIIA, BZ377, RH•F, No.88 Squadron, June 1944**
  Dark Green upper surfaces and Medium Sea Grey undersides; codes in dull red, serial in Night; forward fuselage painted in white distemper and D-Day stripes applied around wings in black and white. Note small 'F' repeated at rear end of fuselage and smoke-laying pipes under the belly

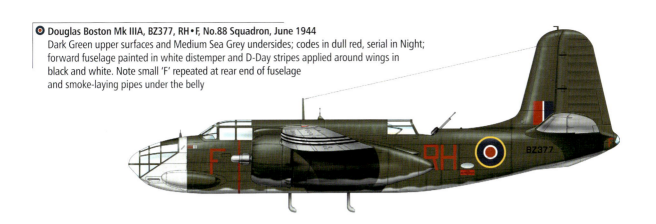

- **Avro Lancaster B Mk III, RF144, EM•H of No.207 Squadron, RAF Spilsby, March 1945**
  Dark Earth/Dark Green upper surfaces with Night undersides; Type C1 roundels on fuselage and Type B roundels above wings (no markings under wings); codes in dull red outlined in yellow; serial in dull red

- **Avro Lancaster B Mk I, ME499, AS•D, No.166 Squadron, RAF Kirmington, Spring 1945**
  High-visibility 'Daylight' markings consisting of yellow wingtips, fins and rudders on this particular Lancaster, though these varied from aircraft to aircraft

- **De Havilland Mosquito NF Mk XIX, MM850, RS•J, No.157 Squadron, RAF Swannington, late 1944**
  Ocean Grey/Dark Green finish with undersides overpainted in Night; black/white stripes around wings and fuselage; Ident Red codes, Night serials

- **Short Stirling Mk IV, LJ981, 8E•C, No.295 Squadron, RAF Harwell (Oxfordshire), 1944**
  Dark Earth/Dark Green upper surfaces with Night undersides; codes and serial in red; Type B roundels above wings

Douglas C-47A

1/72nd
by Libor Jekl

The C-47 Sktrain undertook a vital role during Allied airborne operations for the D-Day landings, and continued as a transport aircraft during operations over continental Europe during the last stages of WWII. Its civil predecessor, the DC-3, substantially influenced the development of air transport in the 1930s not just in the USA but worldwide. The type was built under licence and also copied in the USSR and Japan, but it was the military cargo version that was produced in the greatest numbers, with many being sold after the war to numerous countries to become the foundation of many revived airlines.

The Airfix kit belongs to the latest generation in their production programme and obviously the box art depicting a machine in D-Day marking was very eye-catching. The large box contains five sprues moulded from a light grey-coloured plastic containing more than 120 parts, plus a single clear sprue. Typically for an Airfix kit the sprue attachments are a bit large, but the parts are cleanly moulded without flash or other visible flaws. The number of ejector pin marks is quite high, though, but fortunately these are mostly located in less visible places; anyway, those positioned in the cargo cabin between the ribs may bother some and should therefore be addressed. The surface detail and panel lines are nice and fine, although some examples may suffer from poor quality control, as did my two examples; while the first one was OK, the second one suffered from a gritty surface texture and some of the components were distorted. Delicately moulded are certain raised panels on the fuselage and wings, and equally good is the reasonably subtle fabric effect on the control surfaces. On the other hand, the wing's trailing edge seems to be too thick and needs some sanding to get it to scale. The cockpit and cargo cabin are nicely detailed, although the instrument panel is supplied only as a decal, but that really does not matter because it can hardly be seen anyway. The fuselage windows are

Technical Data	
Airfix 1/72nd Douglas C-47A Skytrain	
Kit No.:	A08014
Material:	IM
Worldwide distributor:	Hornby Hobbies Ltd
UK Price:	£24.99

The ejector pin marks inside the fuselage halves are elegantly filled with the etched discs for this job included in the Eduard photo-etched interior detail set

The floor panel was warped, but it soon straightened with some warm water and a bit of pressure; you can also see the photo-etched parts added in the cockpit area

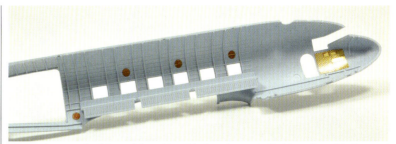

More photo-etched from Eduard is added to the cockpit sidewalls, with the port side shown here

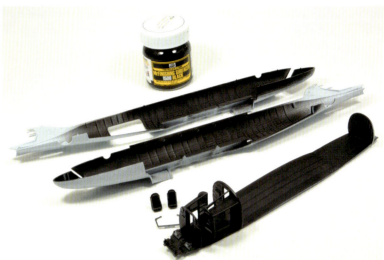

All of the interior is first sprayed with Mr Finishing Surface 1500 Black primer

The interior is then painted with a green Zinc Chromate primer colour, with the aft area by the loading door receiving some 'dirt' effects courtesy of MIG Productions pigments and Pigment Fixer

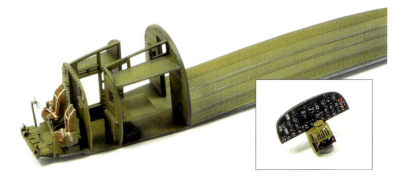

The completed interior section, with the pre-painted instrument panel and seat belts from the Eduard seat added to the cockpit area

moulded together with their outer frame and they are inserted into the fuselage from outside, which seems a little odd, but actually works very well. The undercarriage section offers an array of detailed parts, you even have the oil tanks, engine rear bulkhead and finely moulded struts. The main wheels are moulded 'weighted', but they lack any tread pattern. The engines seem to be the weakest part of the kit, being simplified with plain cylinders without cooling fins or any ancillaries. The kit provides an alternative ski undercarriage applicable to the post-war option, and optional propellers with pointed and 'paddle' style of blades. The presence of other parts that are not used here means that there are most likely other versions in the pipeline, including civilian ones. The decal sheet is printed by Cartograph and is of first class quality, it contains markings for an example of the Military Air Transport Services from Canada in 1949 and the 92nd Troop Carrier Squadron with the nose art 'Kilroy is here', which on 6th June 1944 operated from Uppotery airfield in Devon and which was my choice for this build. I also acquired a number of aftermarket sets that either addressed the simplified nature of some parts or offered good detail and value for money: Quickboost exhaust (#QB72462), propellers (#QB72458) and air intakes (#QB72461), Eduard Brassin wheels (#672 046) and photo-etched interior (#73-513) and exterior (#72-587) detail sets.

Construction

The ejector pin marks in the cargo section could be elegantly addressed with Eduard's etched plugs featured in the interior set, which I glued in place with thin cyanoacrylate and wiped off any residue with cotton buds soaked in debonder. To the fuselage sides I cemented the side consoles with the seats for the troops (the kit also contains the folded version of these) and the roof section with interior lights. With the etched parts enhancing the cockpit sides and floor glued in place, I sprayed the interior with Mr Surfacer 1500 (black), which formed a rich background for the interior colour. I opted for Zinc Chromate I (#351) from CSI Creos (Gunze-Sangyo) Aircraft Interior Color Set #CS681, which I further darkened with black and airbrushed it in several thin coats to achieve good contrast; this is soft in less visible areas and high in the cargo cabin and here I also accentuated the ribs with a lighter shade mixed from Vallejo acrylics. The floor in the cargo cabin was dusted with MIG Production Light Earth pigment and fixed in place with Pigment Fixer and some scratches were added using a silver watercolour pencil. From 0.2mm thin lead foil I cut 27 pairs of seat belts, formed them to shape and painted them in a cream colour (#H318). In the cockpit I added the remaining pre-painted parts such as the instrument panel, side consoles and seat

The etched set does not include lap straps for the cargo area seats, so 27 sets were cut from thin lead foil, then painted and added to each seat

belts and the assembled interior was inserted into the fuselage. In my kit the floor was badly warped, so was levelled out using warm water and adequate force and then all parts fitted inside without problem. Now I could close the fuselage but despite careful trimming on the spine two panel lines did not match , even though all the others did, so these had to be filled with thicker cyanoacrylate and rescribed. The complete fuselage joint was further reinforced with thin cyanoacrylate that at the same time sealed the joint, so it did not 'sink' in the future.

The kit has a unique wing assembly that is divided into seven pieces with separately moulded aerodynamic wing-to-fuselage transitions and a wing spar running through the centre-section that reinforces the complete assembly. I consider this as an advantage as the parts are divided at actual panel lines and that makes the work easier, but on the other hand it requires extremely precise assembly work and flawlessly moulded parts that have no deformities. Anyway, first I dealt with wheel bay interior where I cemented in place the etched reinforcing bands, oil tank caps and various hydraulic lines and ribs. The real assembly starts with installation of the wing spar in the centre-section that is then glued to the fuselage. In order to firmly fix the join I used strong metal clamps and the fit was pretty good except for a 2mm step at one side below the cargo doors that was sanded to shape. During the trial fitting I also reduced the height of the spar under the floor by about 1mm so the wing could correctly sit in the fuselage opening. I continued by installing the transition pieces, secured with extra thin Mr Cement S. Next I had to finish painting the wheel bays as it would not be possible later, then I installed the upper wing halves. On the left side I filled the larger gaps with regular Mr White Putty, rescribed the panel line and continued with the bottom outer halves. Before that I had

Everything ready and placed into one fuselage half

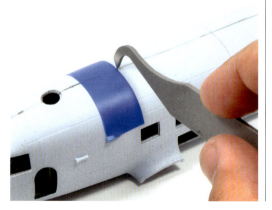

For some odd reason, the two front upper panel lines did not line up, so they were filled and then rescribed

to remove the guide ribs on the inside of the upper halves because these oddly prevented the bottom halves from sitting properly. Despite more work and number of trial assemblies I still consider the design of this assembly as favourable, because it gives excellent rigidity to the whole thing. You are not worried about a fragile and unsatisfactory joint, as I experienced in the past while building Esci and Italeri C-47/DC-3 kits. The wing landing lights were enhanced with glass lenses from fashion jewellery and the clear cover was bordered with the etched rim.

I continued with the assembly of the engine

Here you can see the various etched additions to the engine bulkhead and undercarriage bays

You will need pressure at the front and rear wing/fuselage joint, as seen here thanks to strong metal clamps on the leading edge…

The bulkheads and all detail inside the wings have to be painted and weathered before any assembly take place, as you will never reach these areas once the wings are together

…the same applied to the trailing edge as well to get everything to align and the seams to be good and tight

The engines are basic in the kit, but after painting and the addition of the etched ignition harness from the Eduard set, they are passable

You will have to thin down the interior of the outer wing (lower) panels, to get the spar to fit inside snugly and not spread the wing halves apart

To get the engines to fit into their cowlings, you will have to snip off one of the two lugs inside

The intakes are multi-part in the kit, plus not very accurate, so they were replaced with the single-piece Quickboost examples seen on the right

The cabin windows fit from the outside, and are not the best of fits, whilst the cockpit windscreen is multi-part; the astrodome is left off until after painting

The model is masked up ready for the primer to be applied

The overall primer coat is Mr Surfacer 1000

The invasion stripes go on next, with the black applied first, then the white, as this allows you to use the black underneath to 'shadow shade' the white

Neutral Grey (#H53) is applied to the undersides, with a darkened version used to highlight the panel lines etc.

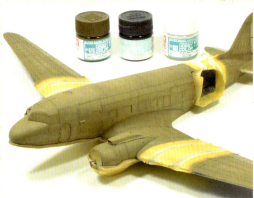

The control surfaces are done with a lightened version of Olive Drab, but also have high and low-lights added as per the main version

The upper surfaces are Olive Drab (#H52) with contrasts achieved by lightening the base colour with white (#H11) or darkening it with Tire Black (#H77); don't use pure black, as that is too intense a colour

The anti-dazzle panel and all the de-icing boots are applied using Flat Black (#N-12) from the new Gunze-Sangyo water-based Acrysion range

The Mid-Green mottling on the wings and tail is done with Dark Green #H320

1/72nd Build – Douglas C-47A Skytrain   Airframe Extra No.1 – D-Day To VE Day

All the decals went on well with the help of Gunze-Sangyo Mr Mark Setter and Mr Mark Softer

The Eduard etched set add a lot of details to the cargo doors, including the access steps

The kit propellers on the left were replaced with the Quickboost ones on the right, simply because the latter had better hub detail and the diameter was correct (e.g. greater)

units and these were sprayed in metallic shades first and then post-shaded with a black mixture, then I added the etched ignition cables. The instructions suggest you join the cowling halves together with the engines and glue them at the same time to the wing, but in my opinion there are too many operations all at once and I suspect sanding any joint lines on the cowling with the engines in would not be very convenient! Therefore I approached this in my usual way and assembled the cowlings first, sorted out any imperfections and only then did I install the engines. However, the engines would have been obstructed by two large fixing slots, so I cut one off then glued the units to the wing. The air intakes with dust filters I replaced with the Quickboost parts because they feature the correct size inlet openings and since they are cast as single pieces, they are a lot easier to work with. Once the tailplanes were fixed in situ I turned my attention to the clear parts. The fuselage windows were snapped in place and fixed with a minimal amount of extra thin glue, and even though they did not fit completely flush with the fuselage surface they look fine on the finished kit. However, the circular apertures for the troops inside to put a gun through are only provided as decals

The undercarriage parts are well moulded, but the kit wheels have no tread pattern and look too 'weighted', so they were replaced with the Brassin resin ones seen here

The undercarriage in situ, note the pigments used to create 'dirt' in the treads

and these looked really awful once applied, so I removed them and left the windows without the 'holes'. The cockpit glazing is split into three parts to allow the side windows to be opened if required, and they eventually fitted well after a little trimming; the navigator's astrodome was installed after the painting stage. All the windows were masked with the Eduard canopy masks, all openings were blocked with foam and the kit received a coat of Mr Surfacer 1000 (grey) primer. Since I had really nice scale drawings with all the rivets shown, I reproduced them using a 'Rosie the Riveter' tool.

Colour

Camouflage for this aircraft consisted of the usual combination of Olive Drab and Neutral Grey with Mid-Green mottling along the wing and tailplane edges; naturally invasion stripes are also applied. The strips went on first and once these were masked off I continued with Neutral Grey underneath (#H53). The base colour was then post-shaded along the panel lines with a darkened version. For the Olive Drab shade I decided on CSI Creos (Gunze-Sangyo) H52 that was lightened with 20% white, while the fabric covered surfaces received a lighter shade with about 30% white. The surface was subsequently post-shaded with lighter and darker variants of

The antennae on each side of the fuselage/nose area were updated with scratchbuilt elements made from stretched sprue

Fuel and oil stains were created by careful application of the applicable wash from the AK Interactive range

Olive Drab mixed from the base colour with addition of white, yellow and black, with the goal of creating not heavy weathering, but an optically 'broken' and non-uniform surface shade. Next I airbrushed the Mid-Green (#H320) patches and at the end I masked off the de-icing boots on the leading edges and sprayed them black (#H12) together with anti-glare panel on the nose and the wing walkways.

After fixing the paints with Gunze-Sangyo GX100 gloss varnish I applied the decals, which were perfectly printed with minimum excess of carrier film and reacted well to the Gunze-Sangyo Mr Mark Setter and Softer decal solutions. Then followed the panel line wash mixed from black and brown oil paints and any excesses were wiped off with cotton buds before the kit was left overnight to dry thoroughly.

Final Details

In the meantime I continued with the landing gear assembly, sprayed the main legs and auxiliary struts with Mr Surfacer 1500 (black) and then with Alclad II Duraluminium. From the main legs it was necessary to cut off part of the outer horizontal axle, which only applies to the ski version, so be warned as this can easily be overlooked in the instructions. From the etched parts I sourced the hydraulic brake lines and I prepared the resin wheels from Brassin. Compared to the kit's wheels they have a tread pattern, beautiful hub details and the tyre 'weighting' seems to be less prominent then on the kit parts. The gear assembly did not pose any issues as the fit is well done via pins and lugs; the single auxiliary strut (#E13) had to be shortened by 2mm, though, in order for it to fit in the opening in the middle

The completed propellers, with the stencils from the kit decals applied

of the oil tank. The wheels need to be inserted in the main struts before cementing the rear fork-type strut, otherwise these could easily be broken off. The tailwheel looked nice, with its separately moulded wheel, and from a piece of self-adhesive silver tape I reproduced the oleo piston. I added antennae masts, but I left off the fork-type one located in front of the astrodome because I believe this was a very late-war (or even post-war) addition because I could not find any photographs confirming it on any C-47 during 1944. The side antennas below the cockpit were replaced with new items scratchbuilt from pieces of stretched sprue. The exhausts from the kit I exchanged with the Quickboost items painted in a metallic shade as a base and then post-shaded with a mix of heavily diluted black and brown. The propeller units were also replaced with resin versions because these had better hub detail and seemed to have a correct (larger) diameter.

After installing the open front and cargo doors I fixed the surface with a light mist of matt varnish (Gunze-Sanyo Mr Color #182) and with AK Interactive Fuel Stains and Engine Oil enamels I brushed on leaks of these fluids around the filling ports and engine cowlings. At the very end I attached the aerial lead made from Uschi van den Rosten fine rigging thread.

Verdict

The Airfix kit offers a modern rendition of this legendary aircraft in 1/72nd scale. The older Esci and Italeri kits in my opinion should not be relegated to the "only for collectors" shelf just yet. The improvement in the surface detail may not be so apparent on first inspection, though, but Airfix at least have not done the rivet lines as engraved lines as was the case with the aforementioned competitors' kits.

Overall, this is very nice kit indeed, but it is a little complex and as such it is more suitable for experienced builders, plus it's also relatively pricey.

References
- C-47 Skytrain In Action No.149 by L. Davis (Squadron/Signal Publications 1995 ISBN: 0-89747-329-9)
- DC-3, Fifty Glorious Years ny Arthur Pearcy, (Airlife)
- DC-3 & C-47 Gooney Birds (Airlife)
- Douglas C-47/DC-3, Famous Airplanes of the World No.66 (Bunrin-do 1975)
- Douglas C-47 & C-53, Italian Monographs No.8 (Monografic Aeronautiche 1981)
- Douglas DC-3 by L. Morgan (Morgan Aviation Books 1965)
- Douglas DC-3, Owners' Workshop Manual by P. Blackah (Haynes Publishing 2011 ISBN: 978-0-7603-4291-6)
- Douglas DC-3 (pre-1942) by A. Pearcy, Profile No.96 (Profile Publications 1966)
- Douglas DC-3 Surviviors by A. Pearcey (Aston Publications Ltd 1988)
- Douglas Dakota Mk I-IV by A. Pearcey, Profile No.220 (Profile Publications 1971)

Spitfire PR Mk XIX

1/72nd

by Libor Jekl

This is one of the better kits from the Airfix brand under Hornby's control and despite simplified detail, thicker panel lines and overall treatment that is more typical of a cheap 'easy kit' it is definitely not a kit that should be left off your display shelves. If we ignore the aged MPM short-run kit from the late 1990s, the Fujimi kit, though from the opposite end of the price spectrum, can't offer precise and accurate details, despite its delicate features typical of a Japanese manufacturer. Therefore the Airfix kit is quite a reasonable choice and a good starting point. The kit provides the late version with the pressurised cockpit (Type 390) and despite simplified detail there seems to be no compromise made on the accuracy, as the kit is pretty much spot on in overall dimensions and proportions. There are a few little things omitted here and there like the missing braces above the wheel bays or the safety valves at the end of the 'bowser' wing, but I think of more concern are the simplified wheel bays that are just simple cut-outs in the wing, plus the oleo legs are moulded together with the doors. The propeller blades are little bit out of shape despite having the right diameter, and the fabric effect on the rudder seems too heavy. The wheels come with two hub styles and they look usable, as does the tailwheel. Also the cockpit details are pretty decent providing the canopy remains closed and that odd-looking pilot figure with a jet style helmet will be omitted. The parts have to be removed from the sprues with care because the gates are too thick and robust. While the canopy seems to be fine albeit a little bit thick, the bottom camera apertures look awful and do not fit in the corresponding holes. I'm sure Spitfire nuts would find many other points for discussion, anyway I think this kit represents very acceptable basis for further work or it can be undertaken purely out of the box as an ideal subject for taking your breath between more demanding projects. This latter comment is certainly supported when you consider the ease

Technical Data
Airfix 1/72nd Supermarine Spitfire PR Mk XI (converted to a Type 389)
Kit No.: A02017
Material: IM
Worldwide distributor: Hornby Hobbies Ltd
UK Price: £7.99

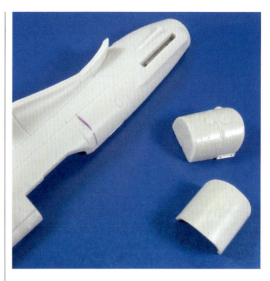
The ArmoryCast Griffon engine set is extremely good

The first job was to cut away the upper decking for the tank, but as this is intended for the Fujimi kit, you actually cut inboard of the panel lines, which are later filled

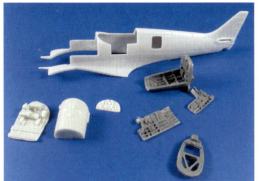

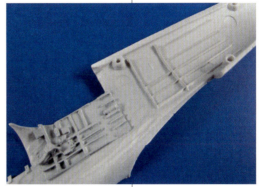
A little extra detail needs to be added in the aft fuselage areas around the camera and this is done with plasticard

With the fuselage interior suitably thinned to accept the new parts, here you can see the ArmoryCast and Pavla resin parts for the cockpit and engine bulkhead

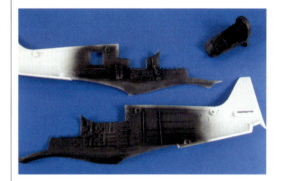
All the interior parts are first sprayed black

of construction; I managed to build one example during a weekend event of our modelling club with the net building time of around 14 hours.

If you really want to go to town with this kit you have quite a few aftermarket sets to choose from. Pavla Models produces three resin sets covering the complete interior including the camera bay and exterior with propeller unit, radiators and landing gear. Quickboost offer a set of

A light application of Interior Grey-Green gives tonal contrast

The instrument panel is enhanced with dial decals

With the fuselage together, you can see the oblique camera in the port side

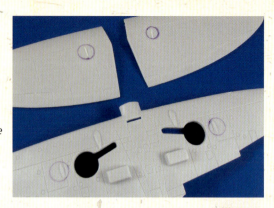

All of these bulges on the kit wings have to be removed when doing the earlier Type 389

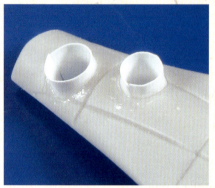

The camera ports in the underside are drilled and then lined with rolls of plasticard

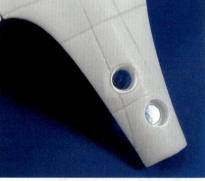

Here you can see the new lenses set in by some 1.5mm

New lenses are punched out of clear plasticard

The wing-to-fuselage joints are not bad, but some filler will still be required

Sadly the main wheel wells are devoid of any sidewalls

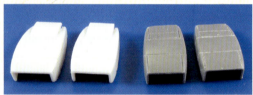

The Pavla radiators (right) are more accurate than the kit ones (left)

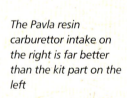

The Pavla resin carburettor intake on the right is far better than the kit part on the left

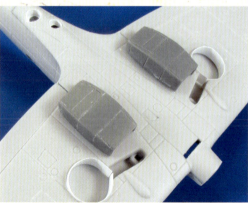

With the new resin radiators in place, you can see the wheel wells being boxed in with strips of plasticard

The vacformed windscreen may not be 100% correct, but it does fit the contours of the kit very well indeed; it is masked up here along with the fixed rear section

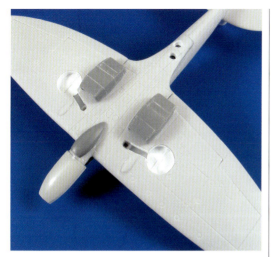

You can see the sidewalls added to the oleo leg sections of each wheel well, along with the strengthening ribs inside each main bay

Once the model is primed, all the rivets are applied with a straight edge and a 'Rosie the Riveter' tool

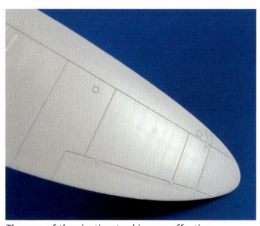

The use of the riveting tool is very effective

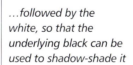

The underside after the base primer is polished smooth

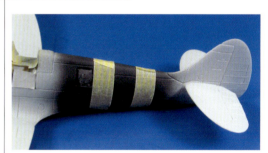

The invasion stripes are created on the fuselage, with the black going on first…

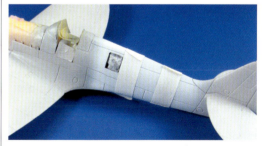

…followed by the white, so that the underlying black can be used to shadow-shade it

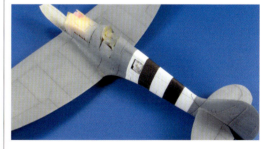

The completed fuselage invasion stripes after the overall PRU Blue has been put on

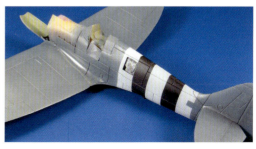

A coat of gloss varnish is applied in preparation for the decals

exhausts and the canopy masking is a lot easier thanks to the Eduard masks. Alternative markings can be found on Xtradecal (12 options in total for RAF and Turkish examples) or Freightdog (PS888 'The Last') decal sheets.

Construction

I intended to take on my second Mk XIX kit build with a more 'experimental' attitude and convert it to a Type 389 and at the same time utilise the available aftermarket sets; as a real challenge I eventually also decided on the Armycast engine set that is intended for the Fujimi kit. This set consists of about twenty beautifully cast parts and offers the complete Griffon installation from the rear face of the instrument panel up to the spinner. I therefore started the build by measuring the corresponding parts and checking the cross section of the engine bulkhead, which thankfully matched the Airfix kit fuselage almost perfectly. Compared to the Fujimi kit there is about 1.5 mm difference in the length of the upper fuselage part where the fuel tank is located, so I had to make the cuts outside the panel lines and these were subsequently filled in with thick cyanoacrylate glue. With a razor saw I removed the cowling panels and the cockpit side doors (these were used only on the early Type 389 with the non-pressurised cockpit). The fuselage walls were thinned at corresponding places with the Dremel tool and all was levelled and sanded

The markings came from an Xtrdecal sheet and settled down into the recessed details well with a bit of Micro Set and Sol solutions

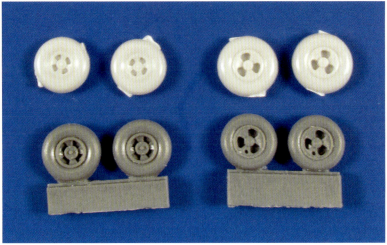

Both types of main wheel hub are offered in the replacement wheels included in the Pavla Models exterior set

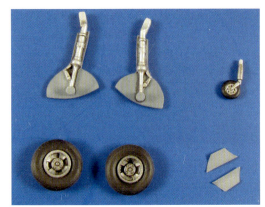

Although the oleo legs and doors are moulded together, once painted and a dark wash applied, they looked quite acceptable

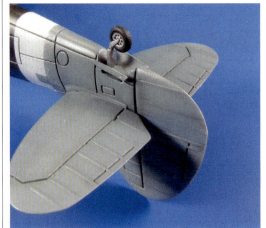

The tailwheel doors were replaced with new ones made from thin aluminium sheet

smooth with sanding sticks. Now I trial-fitted dimension-wise all the important resin parts such as the engine bulkhead, fuel tank and the cockpit tub in the fuselage and made any necessary corrections; generally the fit was surprisingly good. The outlet for the cockpit over-pressure valve behind the canopy was sanded off and the rear fuselage around the camera received spars cut from thin plastic stock. The Pavla Models camera set offers two F.52 and one F.24 camera, but I used only the latter oblique mounted camera as the supporting structure of the rest corresponds to the later style installation. As far as the camera configuration is concerned, the vertical F.52s were not used together with the F.24; according to the aircraft operation manual only the F.24s could be used in all three mountings together, with the other set-ups being combinations of F.52 and F.8 cameras. From the rear cockpit bulkhead I removed the bottle that was part of the anti-moisture system (installed on the Type 390 only) and all the resin parts were primed with Mr Surfacer 1200 (grey) applied from a can. The interior was sprayed with a base black colour on which several thinned coats of Interior Grey-Green (GSI Mr Color #364) went on in different densities to simulate contrast, especially in the fuselage rear area. The instrument panel was improved with Mike Grant instrument faces decals and the details were picked out with Vallejo acrylics. The seat belts were sourced from an Eduard pre-coloured set and the camera lens was imitated using dark blue and a drop of gloss varnish.

While the fuselage was set aside for drying, in the meantime I worked on the wing. From the wing bottom surface I cut off the covers of the fuel pumps because these are only correct for the late version, above the wheel wells I added the stiffeners cut from suitable plastic stock and also the safety valve lines at the wing tips. The oddly shaped camera apertures were completely replaced with pieces of rolled plastic strips that were glued in the holes, sanded smooth and glazed about 1.5mm under the surface level. A very useful tool here is a punch and die set because it can produce the ring and clear disc of the required diameter. The wing-to-fuselage joint was not completely trouble free, but a few drops of cyanoacrylate glue sorted out any gaps. The empty wheel bays were boxed in with a strip of plasticard and the internal ribs were cut from the same material. The Pavla Models radiators look better than the kit items, especially their height is much closer to the real thing and they also feature nice louvre detail. They are designed as direct replacement, so they just need to be fitted onto the wing. The cast carburettor intake features much finer detail too, as the inlet is correctly shaped with thin edges. Next I fitted the bottom part of the engine cowling and that needed a little filling and sanding to get the right

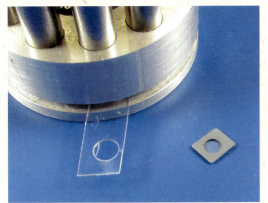

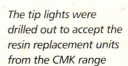
The tip lights were drilled out to accept the resin replacement units from the CMK range

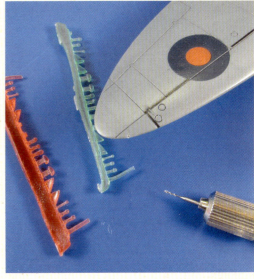

The camera access door in the fuselage side had the centre port glazed with a disc of clear plastic

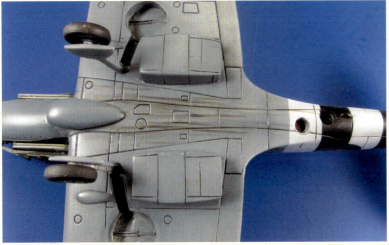

The oil streaks on the underside were done with a suitable medium from the AK Interactive range

The CMK light in situ in the port wing tip

A little light pigment from the MIG productions range was added to the main wheel wells

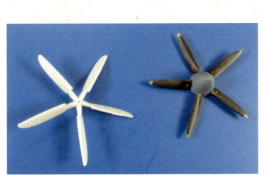

The kit propeller (left) is best replaced with the resin one in the Pavla exterior set (right)

All the various sub-assembles prior to final assembly

profile because it is designed for the Fujimi kit that is a different shape in this area. Also the total length of this part differs slightly and needed trimming once the engine had been installed. The main airframe assembly continued with the vacformed replacement canopy, which was cut into three parts. The shape of the windshield seems to correspond to the late version, as it is flatter at the front, but I used it anyway - at least it matched perfectly the fuselage contour. All of the engine compartment was brushed black to avoid any light showing through, and using a fine toothbrush any dust and other particles were removed from the surface. The clear parts were all masked off and all apertures filled before a primer coat of Mr Surfacer 1000 (grey) was applied. The surface of the kit was subsequently riveted, sanded with fine wet and dry and polished with sticks to a high shine.

Colour

I went for RM643 '•Z' that I found on the Xtradecal sheet, which was used by No.541 Squadron at RAF Benson in late 1944. The camouflage of this machine consisted of the usual PRU Blue overall with D-Day stripes applied on the fuselage. Once these were sprayed on and masked off the PRU Blue followed; as there is no equivalent shade among my favourite Gunze-Sangyo paints I had to dig in my paint stock and pull out an old bottle of Aeromaster PRU Blue (1117) that was surprisingly in good condition after about 15 years! Once thinned with Tamiya acrylic thinners it worked perfectly. Since this sort of aircraft was usually kept in almost pristine condition, I did not apply much weathering, only a few high and low lights sprayed as darker patches along the panel lines. A few paint scratches on the wing root were added with a silver Prismacolor pencil and the gloss varnish was applied to seal the surface before the decal application.

The Xtradecal sheet is printed with excellent quality and all the individual decals have good colour, density and register. They worked flawlessly with the help of a few drops of Microscale Set and Sol solution, while the walkways decals and few stencils were sourced from my decal bank.

Final Details

Now I could put the Spitfire on its own legs. The main gear struts are moulded with the doors and do not look that good, but after painting them and applying the dark wash they looked usable, thus my 'Plan B' to utilise complete units from the spares box did not happen. Anyway the wheels were replaced with the Pavla items that offer delicate hub detail and are of accurate diameter. The tailwheel's retractable covers were cut from thin aluminium foil and shaped according to the original parts.

With the undercarriage added I could proceed with the final engine unit assembly. First, the primed resin parts were sprayed in corresponding

shades: the fuel, oil and glycol tank in Aluminium, the engine itself received black followed by Testor's Metalizer Exhaust, which was polished to a semi-gloss lustre, while the cowlings were painted Interior Grey-Green. I prepared several diameters of lead wire that were brush-painted in black, aluminium, light grey and brass and these were bent to the required shape ready to be installed. The engine was then glued into the fuselage; its rear part is supported by the carburettor intake duct, so it is not difficult to set up the correct position in the fuselage. The front part was fixed with the plate glued into the glycol tank and the engine's position was set with the bearers and the side bars with the exhausts. The cowling fixtures were sourced from a Griffon etched set and glued along the engine bay. Now I added all the 'mess' of piping and wiring with the pre-painted lead wires using several pictures of the Mk XIX Griffon installation as a guide. Once completed the engine compartment was dry-brushed with light grey oil paint to pick out the details and a heavy diluted dark wash was applied on the main engine components as well.

After a sealing coat of semi-matt varnish I glued the remaining bits, the cockpit hood, aerial, IFF antenna, pitot tube and the propeller, which was assembled from the Pavla set. The camera cover panel was cut out of thin plasticard and the aperture punched out and glazed with a clear disc. At the very end I applied AK Interactive Fuel Stains around the fuel caps, whilst 'Engine Oil' from the same manufacturer reproduced the oil stains on the wing underside centre section. The wheel bays were slightly dusted up with MIG Production Light European Earth pigment brushed in the bays and sealed with MIG thinners. The wingtip lights were drilled out and replaced with CMK lights cast from coloured resin.

Verdict

This was a very enjoyable build indeed and despite its complexity it was relatively easy and straightforward. The Airfix kit is acceptably detailed despite being simplified in places, but it builds very well. The Pavla Model sets are valuable improvements indeed, especially the cockpit and exterior sets are very welcome choices if you want to improve the most basic areas of the kit. I also noticed quite an improvement in the quality of casting in these sets in comparison with previous products from Pavla. The Armycast set is excellent value for money too, as they are almost on a bar with the major resin aftermarkets players, plus there is no other Griffon engine set available on the 1/72nd market.

References
- Spitfire PR Mk XIX - Air Publication 1565W
- Spitfire The History by E.B. Morgan & E. Shacklady (Key Publishing 1987 ISBN: 0-946219-48-6)
- Supermarine Spitfire PR Mk XIX by R. Theiner (MPM Publications Ltd 1995)
- Vickers-Supermarine Griffon Spitfires, Aero Detail No.30 (Dai Nippon Kaiga Co., Ltd 2001 ISBN: 4-499-22741-0)

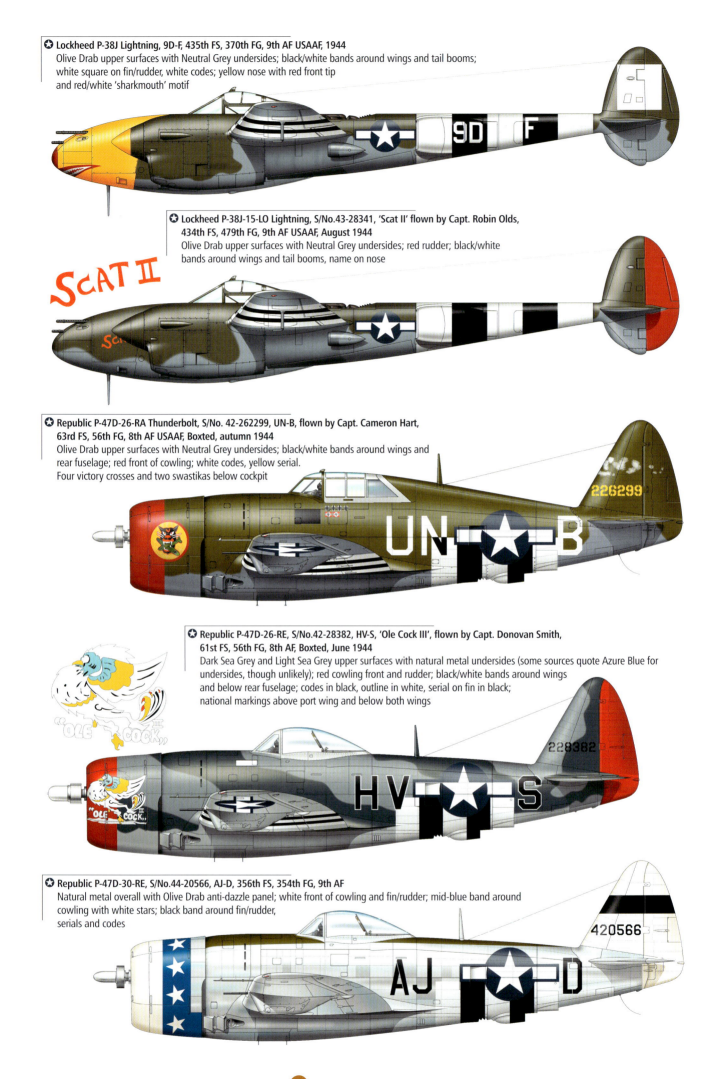

✪ **North American P-51B-7-NA Mustang, S/No.43-6833, FT-O, 'Beantown Banshee' flown by Capt. Felix M. Rogers, 353rd FS, 354th FG, 9th AF USAAF, summer 1944**
Natural metal overall with Olive Drab anti-dazzle panel; yellow spinner and black band around nose; black/white bands around wings and rear fuselage; name in yellow, roughly outlined in Olive Drab; codes and serials in black. Four victory markings in black, outlined in yellow

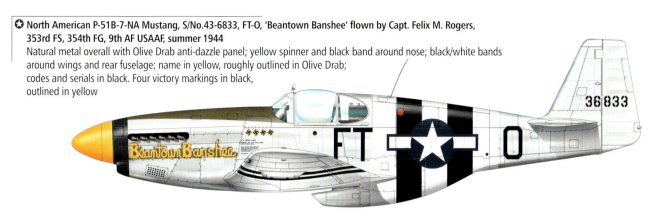

✪ **North American P-51B-5-NA Mustang, S/No.43-6935/C5-T, 'Hurry Home Honey', flown by Capt. Richard Peterson, 364th FS, 357th FG, 8th AF, USAAF, May 1944**
Olive Drab ANA 613/Sea Grey ANA 603 upper surfaces with Light Grey ANA 602 undersides; yellow/red checks and bands around nose; black/white bands around wings and rear fuselage; white codes (with '5' outlined in black), yellow serial; lettering and mission markings/kills in white

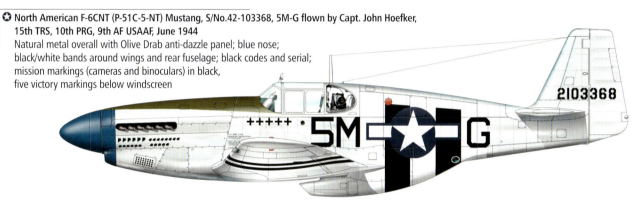

✪ **North American F-6CNT (P-51C-5-NT) Mustang, S/No.42-103368, 5M-G flown by Capt. John Hoefker, 15th TRS, 10th PRG, 9th AF USAAF, June 1944**
Natural metal overall with Olive Drab anti-dazzle panel; blue nose; black/white bands around wings and rear fuselage; black codes and serial; mission markings (cameras and binoculars) in black, five victory markings below windscreen

✪ **North American P-51B-15-NA Mustang, S/No.42-106872, PE-T (bar), flown by 1st Lt John F. Thornell Jr, 328th FS, 352nd Fighter Group, Bodney, July 1944**
Natural metal overall with blue nose section (thinly outlined in white); codes and serial in black; Night/white 'D-Day' stripes around wings and below rear fuselage; 20 victory markings below cockpit

✪ **North American P-51D Mustang, S/No.44-13334, G4-U, 'Wee WIlly' flown by Capt. Harry Mace, 357th Fighter Group, 362nd Fighter Squadron, 8th Air Force**
Natural metal overall except for the fuselage top decking, horizontal and vertical tail surfaces, which are in Olive Drab; yellow serial on fin, and yellow/red trim on nose; four victory markings beneath canopy

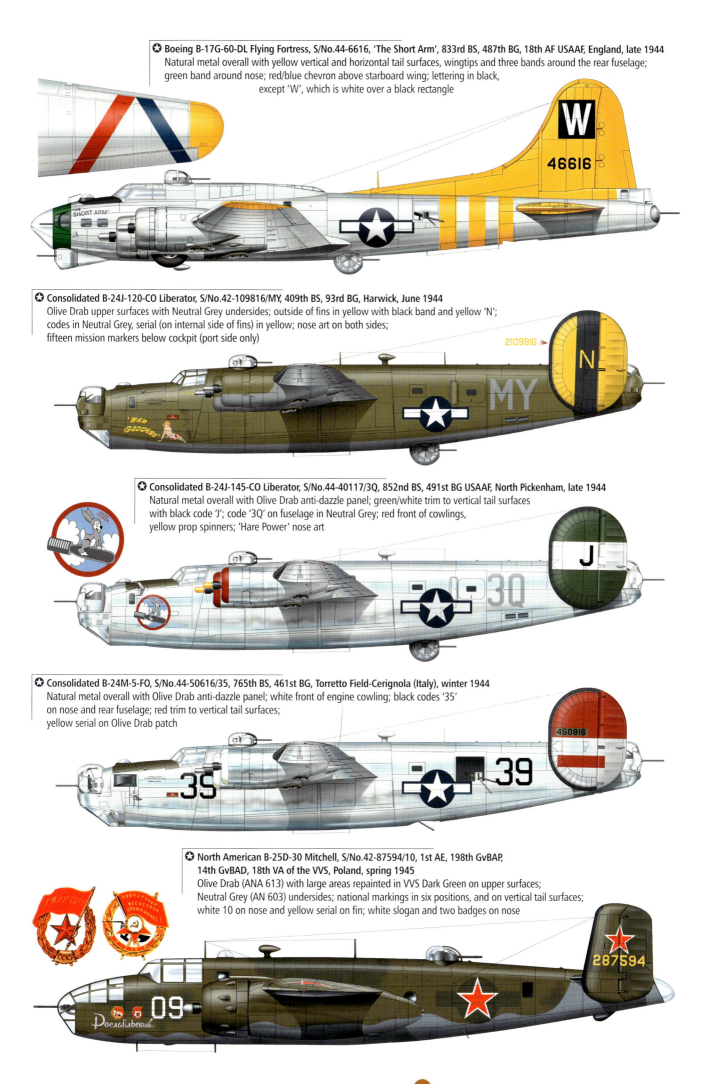

✪ **Martin B-26-50-MA Marauder, S/No.42-95894, K9-P, 'Georgia's On My Mind', 494th BS, 344th BG, 9th Air Force USAAF**
Natural metal overall; Olive Drab on upper surfaces of wings and tailplane, fuselage spine and vertical tail surfaces with Medium Green blotches applied to edges of flying surfaces; code in black, serial in yellow; white triangle on vertical tail surfaces. Aircraft name in red, outlined in white, on an Olive Drab patch on port side only; mission markings in black. On two different photos the aircraft displays yellow/black checks on front of port cowling and none on starboard

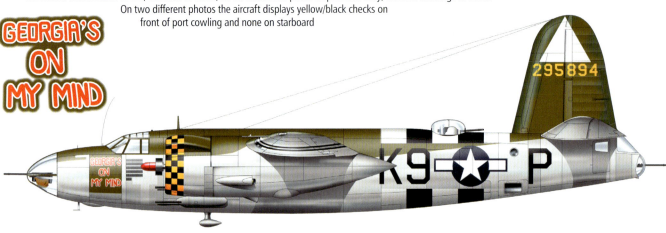

✪ **Douglas A-20J, S/No.43-9913, 8U-A, Squadron Commander's aircraft, 646th BS, 410th BG, June 1944**
Olive Drab and Neutral Grey, with black/white D-Day stripes around rear fuselage and wings. Serial is yellow while codes are white

✪ **Douglas A-26C Invader, S/No.43-22337, 2A-D, 669th BS, 416th BG, 9th Air Force, January 1945**
Natural metal overall with Olive Drab anti-dazzle panel ahead of the cockpit; squadron colour black painted on rudder trailing edge; black/white invasion stripes applied under fuselage only

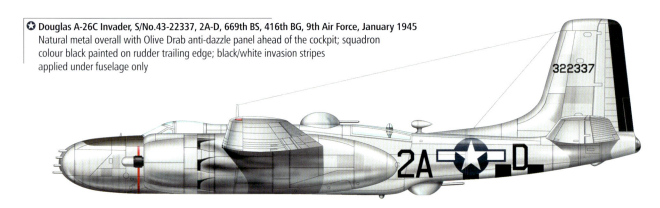

✪ **Martin B-26B-55 Marauder, S/No.42-96165, 6B-T, 'The Big, Hairy Bird', 599th BS, 397th BG, 9th Air Force, England, June 1944**
Natural metal overall with black serials and codes; black/white stripes around wings and rear fuselage; yellow band, outlined in black on fin/rudder; yellow/black/red/white sharkmouth motif with Olive Drab top fuselage, 'hair' aft of cabin canopy and white bull's horns aft of cockpit

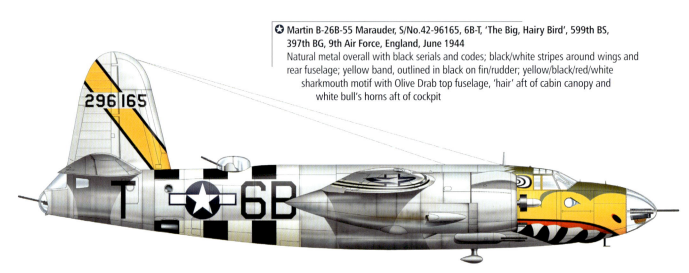

Colour Reference

With so many colours and so many paint manufacturers nowadays, we thought that you might like the following cross-reference chart for the major shades relating to Luftwaffe, RAF and USAAF operations during this final stages of WWII.

Acrylics

Luftwaffe

GS Mr Aqueous	Lifecolor	Tamiya	Xtracrylix	Luftwaffe
H70	UA071	XF-22	XA1201	RLM 02 Grau
H413	UA140	-	XA1213	RLM 04 Gelb
H414	-	-	XA1217	RLM 23 Rot
-	-	-	XA1218	RLM 24 Dunkelblau
H67	UA061	XF-23	XA1202	RLM 65 Hellblau
H416	UA133	-	XA1203	RLM 66 Schwarzgrau
H65	UA051	XF-13*	XA1204	RLM 70 Schwarzgrün
H64	UA052	XF-61	XA1205	RLM 71 Dunkelgrün
-	-	-	XA1222	RLM 72 Grun
H309	UA001	XF-27	XA1223	RLM 73 Grun
H68	UA072	-	XA1206	RLM 74 Graugrün
H69	UA073	-	XA1207	RLM 75 Grauviolett
H417	UA074	-	XA1208	RLM 76 Lichtblau
H421	UA053	-	XA1210	RLM 81 Brunviolett
H422	UA132+	-	XA1212+	RLM 82 Lichtgrün
H423	UA054+	-	XA1211+	RLM 83 Dunkelgrün

* Close approximation
+ Listed as 'RLM 82 Dunkelgrün' or 'RLM 83 Lichtgrün' due to confusion between RLM 82 and 83

RAF

GS Mr Aqueous	Lifecolor	Tamiya	Xtracrylix	RAF
H330	UA091	XF-80	XA1001	Dark Green BS241
H335	UA094	XF-83	XA1003	Medium Sea Grey BS637
H331	UA108	-	XA1004	Dark Sea Grey BS638
H333	-	-	XA1005	Extra Dark Sea Grey BS640
-	UA093	XF-82	XA1006	Ocean Grey
H74	UA095	XF-21	XA1007	Sky BS210
-	-	-	XA1008	PRU Blue BS636
-	-	-	XA1010	Interior Grey-Green

USAAF

GS Mr Aqueous	Lifecolor	Tamiya	Xtracrylix	USAAF
H52	UA005	XF-62	XA1112	Olive Drab ANA 613
H53	UA046	XF-53	XA1133	Neutral Grey
H302	UA008	-	XA1114	Medium Green
H305	-	XF-24	-	Sea Grey ANA 603
H332	-	XF-20	XA1015	Light Grey ANA 602•
-	-	-	-	Insignia Yellow
-	-	XF-7	-	Insignia Red
-	UA134	-	-	Yellow Zinc Chromate Primer
H58	-	-	XA1117	Green Chromate Primer

Note that all Lifecolor paints are matched to the American Federal Standard, so are therefore only approximations for Luftwaffe, British and WWII USAAF colours, which were all made to other colour specifications

• This colour is quoted as being similar to the RAF colour Light Aircraft Grey BS381C 627, so the quoted matches for this colour are in fact RAF Light Aircraft Grey

Colour tabs are for illustration purposes only

Enamels

Luftwaffe

Humbrol	Revell	Xtracolor
240	362	X201 & X409
-	-	X213
-	37	X217
-	-	X218
65	-	X202
32	69	X203
241	46	X204
242	68	X205
243	-	X222
244	67	X223
245	77	X206
246	-	X207
247	49	X208
251	-	X210
252	-	X212+
253	-	X211+

+ Listed as 'RLM 82 Dunkelgrün' or 'RLM 83 Lichtgrün' due to confusion between RLM 82 and 83

RAF

Humbrol	Revell	Xtracolor
163	-	X1
165	-	X3
164	-	X4
-	-	X5
106	-	X6
23	59	X7
-	-	X8
-	-	X10

USAAF

Humbrol	Revell	Xtracolor
66	-	X112
-	374	X133
-	-	X114
-	-	-
166 or 129	-	X15
154	-	X106
153	-	X103
-	-	X408
226	-	X117

• This colour is quoted as being similar to the RAF colour Light Aircraft Grey BS381C 627, so the quoted matches for this colour are in fact RAF Light Aircraft Grey

N.B. We have not included White Ensign Models' Colour Coat series, because at the time of writing, the range no longer existed

Bf 109G-10

1/48th

by Steve A. Evans

Hasegawa have re-released this kit dozens of times with a multitude of versions, and why not? The diminutive fighter from Messerschmitt was created in a bewildering array of variants and it seems only logical that the modelling world should follow suit. This particular box is for the night-fighter version from NJG 11 so you get the glorious all-over RLM 76 schemes and white numbers. The box art is gorgeous and the plastic hidden beneath has been one of the best Bf 109s available in this scale for years. It's pretty generic, mind you, made with the intention of being able to get multiple versions from the least number of moulds. This means some modifications along the way but all are pointed out in the instructions. The plastic is light grey-coloured and well formed, with crisp moulding and almost zero flash. With only half a dozen sprues in the box the parts count isn't very high but what you do get builds relatively easily into a truly iconic aircraft model.

It starts with the interior, which is a simple arrangement of just ten parts, all of which fit neatly and under some RLM 66 paint look quite neat. There is a decal for the instrument panel but the detail in the plastic is easily good enough to paint, if you'd prefer. The only downside is the missing fuel pipe that runs along the starboard sidewall. I've no idea why Hasegawa missed out this obvious feature but it's easy enough to replicate with some clear stretched sprue and careful painting. Other than that, all you need are some seat belts and it's a perfectly acceptable cockpit.

The fuselage is closed without the cockpit tub, which gets inserted from the underside a little later. The centreline joint is neat and tidy and the plastic pretty faithfully re-creates the asymmetric engine cowling of this particular version. You get the larger supercharger air intake to attach and the upper gun cowl is a reasonable fit, although care is needed getting it to line up properly.

Then it's on to the wings and it's here that you get some modifications and options, with upper wing bulges of varying styles, new panel

Stunning box top art, as always from Hasegawa

Technical Data
Hasegawa 1/48th Messerschmitt Bf 109G-10 'NJG 11'
Kit No.: 09771
Material: IM
UK Importer: Ripmax Ltd
UK Price: OOP

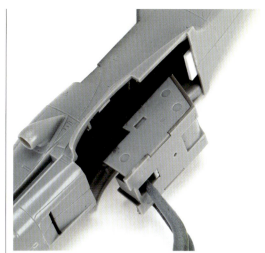

The completed tub slots into place from underneath. Note also here you can see the support plate for the wing-to-fuselage joint. Vital!

lines to scribe and wheel well openings that need trimming. None of this is difficult and the wings themselves fit very well, especially if you put a little support plate into the underside of the fuselage, to keep the single-piece lower wing aligned.

The only other modification you need to do is to extend the exhaust shields down a little to get the anti-glare type used on the night-fighters. The instructions give you some help here but to be honest it's easier to make some new ones out of scrap etched fret. Also, if you're doing the night-fighter versions you need to add a tiny, semi-circular rear-view mirror to the top of the windscreen frame and etch a small rectangular 'clear view' panel on the port side of the canopy. Apparently the Erla hood was plagued with internal reflections at night, so the pilot needed a way to get some clarity of vision.

All the wing control surfaces are separate and they have to be really, because you need to get the radiator flaps in the right position when it's on the ground. Check your reference material to see how they all droop at different angles. You can also cut the elevators free to angle them as well if you like, because that's another very simple modification. With the tail on and the canopy in place to mask the interior, it's time for paint.

The cockpit is reasonable but you have to make the fuel flow indicator pipe yourself

Colour

I was surprised to see three variants in this box, not only the two RLM 76 machines but also one in full camouflage from JG 52, which is interesting because it has the RLM 04 Gelb Luftflotte 4 identification band around the nose. That was never going to be a viable option for me though because I wanted a grey one. The two in the box are virtually identical except for the tactical numbers, one '43' the other '44'. Both have black spinners with white spirals and although it's not shown in the markings and painting guide, both machines should also have the wing fillet filled in with matt black to hide the exhaust staining. My paint of choice is White Ensign Colourcoats RLM 76, which isn't too blue, and applied over a coat of Halfords Grey Plastic Primer it looks smooth and just dying to be scruffed up. Weathering is such an emotive subject of course, because some people love it whilst others go for the more pristine look. I, as usual, opted for the rather dirty end of that particular stick and the following applications of pastel dust, Tamiya X-19 Smoke and pencil paint chips, had this little model looking pretty beaten up in no time. Sealed in under some Johnson's Klear it was time for the decals.

Love them or loathe them, Hasegawa de-

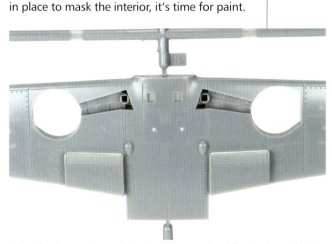

The wheel opening needs to be square edged for the late Bf 109s. The unmodified round one is on the left

You have to do a bit of scribing on the wing upper surface to get the panel lines right for this version

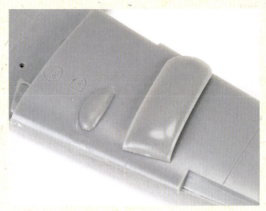

Two styles of wing bulge, the larger one is for the bigger, fatter tyres

The radiators are about as simple as you can get but considering how little of them you can see on the finished item, that's forgiveable

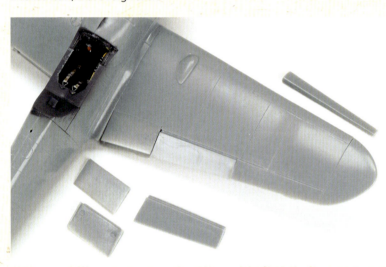

The deeper, larger radiator in the nose needs a little actuator rod put into place. Some stretched sprue will do nicely here

Good to see fully separate controls and flaps on this kit as it makes a huge difference to the way this looks on the ground

The elevators are really simple to cut free as well; just a few scores of a sharp knife and they're loose

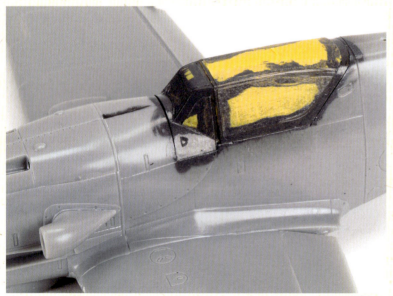

The canopy is the later Erla type and its fit isn't the best but that's OK as it'll be open at the end

Halfords best grey and this gives a good hint at what it will look like in a single colour

cals have always had good and bad points to consider. First, the good; they look great, with excellent printing, colour density and register, they are usually fairly tough so they don't break up too easily and the design is almost always spot on. Now the bad: they take ages to release from the backing paper, they are a little on the thick side and they love to 'silver'. Worse yet is their unpredictable reaction to many softening solutions. You need to get the decal in exactly the right spot before applying any softener because the transfer will literally disintegrate if you touch it after application. Worse yet, sometimes the decals will never settle down properly again, tiny wrinkles remaining on show. Thankfully, there are not many to apply and they managed to behave themselves this time and there are even swastikas on the sheet, so it's not all doom and gloom.

Final Details

After that, the final bits and pieces are applied, which include the undercarriage units, which have reasonable attachment points but you still have to be careful about the odd, 'splayed out'

These bits are the delicate bits that I would have trashed if I'd fitted them earlier. The only additions from me are the brake lines

White Ensign RLM 76 is a glorious shade of slightly scruffy blue/grey. With a few of the panels picked out in a lighter shade it's beginning to look rather nice

I decided to go mucky with this one, so that's lots of exhaust staining and pastel dust to make it look well lived in

look to the legs. The only additional bits will be the usual hydraulic lines on the main legs (fuse wire) and the aerial wires (fishing line) with the other sticky-out bits all provided for you in the kit. The final finish is Xtracolor XDFF Flat Varnish and dark brown matt enamel for the exhaust staining, and it's done.

Verdict

The Hasegawa version of this aircraft has been around for a long time and to be honest, it deserves to be on the shelves because it is arguably still the best available in this scale. You can be sure that none of the other kit manufacturers will be able to match the bewildering number of versions created by Hasegawa, and the simplicity of the kit and the build hide the fact that it is a very accomplished piece of plastic. From complete novice to master builder, everyone can find something worthwhile in these little boxes.

Airframe

& Miniature
Series Titles – 7

Album
Series Titles – 6

Constructor
Series Titles – 2

Detail
Series Titles – 2

Extra
Quarterly

Full details at
www.valiant-wings.co.uk

P-38 Lightning

1/48th

by Steve A. Evans

I must admit, I have something of a soft spot for big, twin-engined aircraft. Many of these are iconic types such as the Beaufighter, Mosquito and Bf 110 but I wonder if any of them can hold a candle to the amazing shape of the P-38? There a number of models out there of the type in all the scales but this particular box from Academy has to be one of the most versatile. Even after 20 years (their original 1/48th P-38 was released in 1994) this particular box still fetches a premium price and looking at the lid is enough to tell you why. Not only can you produce the standard fighter P-38J version, but in there you also get the parts for the bombsight equipped Droopsnoot, the radar nosed Pathfinder and the camera nose of the F-5E. The parts themselves are held on eight sprues of light grey-coloured plastic with a single one of clear bits. The detail is good, without being overdone and whilst there are only a few rivets on the external surfaces, the panel lines are crisp and fully engraved. You also get a very nice decal sheet with four separate versions and with this being an older kit there are literally hundreds of aftermarket decal sheets out there to choose from. The sprues are laid out in a reasonably logical manner, with all the separate versions on their own little extensions. There are even parts on there for making the earlier 'F' and the night-fighter 'M' (a boxing of which I have waiting in the attic), so you can see that Academy really covered all the bases with their plastic P-38s. The only downsides for me about the kit parts are the slight over-simplifying of many of the details and rubber tyres, although these are moulded in a very hard version of that material so they're easier to work with. As an indicator of the vintage nature of the kit, you even get a small tube of poly cement in the box; how quaint.

This particular box contains the bits for the Standard fighter as well as the Droopsnoot, Pathfinder and Recon versions; excellent stuff

Technical Data
Academy 1/48th P-38 Lightning
Kit No.: #12282 (previously #2215 or #FA214)
Material: IM, RB
UK Importer: Pocketbond Ltd
UK Price: £18.99

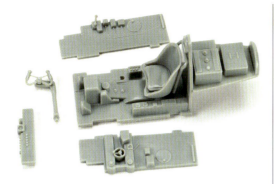

The cockpit interior is pretty good with some nice detail but missing the throttle quadrant and seat belts

That doesn't look too bad, does it? Zinc Chromate interior and homemade belts give it that 'All American' feel

The completed tub nestles neatly into the central nacelle. Apparently this was a very comfortable aircraft to fly

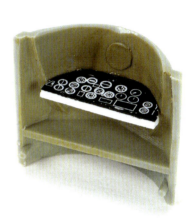

The disappointing instrument panel is not only a rudimentary decal but is also positioned way too far forward. Here you see a plastic card replacement

Construction is entirely logical for such an odd shaped machine and for the most part the fit and finish of all the parts is very good. Parts location is clear enough on the instructions and everything seems to fit just about where it's supposed to. It all starts with the cockpit, which is reasonably detailed, although it's lacking the throttles and mixture levers and the instrument panel is a poor little decal. The location of the main instrument panel is also way too far forward but as you're not going to see much of that on the finished item that's not a huge problem. The completed cockpit sits into the large, single-piece lower fuselage and wing section and the equally impressive upper wing section slips over the top of it. Before closing them up, you must thin out the trailing edges, especially the sections outboard of the engines, otherwise you end up with a hideous looking gap along the wing trailing edge. The engine nacelles and tail booms are moulded with a vertical split and some lovely detail around the tail, with the simple wheel bays trapped between the halves. There's a lot more detail that you could do here but what you get in the kit is a good basic foundation. The undercarriage legs are very neatly done however and all they need is a hydraulic line for the brakes. A bad point for the engine nacelles is the front section with the oil cooler intakes, which is a little fatter than the nacelle itself and doesn't join along any panel line. This means filler, sanding and rescribing, which is not difficult, but it is annoying. It's exactly the same story for the fit of the nacelles to the wings, once again the joints don't pay any attention to where the panel lines are, which would have made it so much easier. Oh well, back out with the filler and sanding sticks.

So, what about those noses, then? Well, as mentioned, you get four versions to play with and to be honest only the standard fighter nose is without problems. All of the other options are completely void of internal detail. Yes, you get a bombsight for the Droopsnoot but there's nothing else. This means that the seat, electronics and control gear that is crammed into the nose is completely absent. It's the same for the Path-

The wing trailing edges need some serious thinning out to get them to close properly

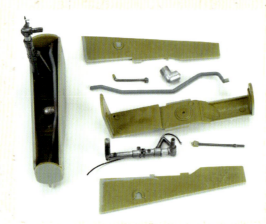

The interior of each wheel well is made up of only a few parts but all the basics are there

This means a lot of filling and sanding is required, followed as always by scribing the correct panel lines into place

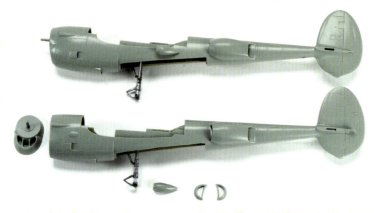

The engines and tail booms are again quite simple but the nosepiece joints don't relate to any panel lines

And which nose would Sir be requiring today? The recon version? A fine choice

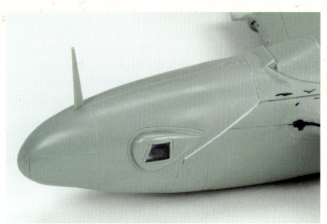

Not a great fit here, as it needed a thin piece of plastic card (10 thou) to take out the gap

The booms and tail all get assembled together and then left alone to set for a good few hours.

Full set of colours, including invasion stripes and strategically lightened panels mean it's getting to look interesting

Once again, the joints don't follow any panel lines, which just makes everything that much harder

Look at that lot! The sticky-out bits on this one seem to go on forever

finder, with no radar gear or seat and the recon version has no cameras. This means that if you intend doing any of these versions, you'll have a bit of scratch-building to do to make some interiors. Don't forget that whichever version you end up choosing, you need to find some room for about 20g of weight to keep the nosewheel on the floor. I had intended to do the F-5E camera ship right from the beginning and all I did was paint the camera lenses on the lower transparencies and blanked off the oblique facing cameras on the inside with some painted plasticard. This also left plenty of room for lead shot to keep the tail up. The fit of the nose section is not great either, with plenty of filling and even an insert of thin plastic card along one of the joints to take up the gaps. At least the shape of this one is reasonably accurate, unlike the Pathfinder nose, which is far too tapered and should be a much more bulbous cross section. All that is needed then is for the horizontal tail to be fitted and the transparencies added and it's time for paint.

Colour

The four options in the box are all very nice and nothing at all like I wanted. Isn't that typical? But that's what the aftermarket people are counting on and in this case I wanted a blue one, so I dug out the AeroMaster decal sheet #48-546. This has some very nice F-5Es, all in the Synthetic Haze colour scheme with invasion stripes and nose art; what's not to love about that?

Painting begins with a good primer to key in the surface and highlight any areas that need some attention before the topcoats go on. This scheme is pretty straightforward with Humbrol 157 Azure Blue being the closest I could find to the Base Sky Blue of the original. This was accompanied by Humbrol 65 Aircraft Blue, for the Flight Blue counter shading on the underside. Various small panels were highlighted with lighter shades of the original colours and the invasion stripes applied. The stripes were done as a full wrap-around of the tail booms, then masked off and the upper portions oversprayed with the Azure Blue, leaving just a hint of them showing.

The basic weathering was then carried out

Painting begins with primer, Halfords best of course, which shows all the little bits that need final blending in before the top coats go on

Synthetic Haze #1: Base Sky Blue, roughly equivalent to FS35123 or Humbrol 157 Azure Blue. What a lovely colour

Synthetic Haze #2: Flight Blue FS35190 (or FS35102 depending on who you believe) via Humbrol 65

with paint chips, pastel dust and Tamiya Smoke, remembering that the worn bits are mostly around the central nacelle where the crew and fitters clamber up onto the wing and the dirty bits will be around the big engines.

After that the Johnson's Klear is applied to get the surface ready for the decals. The kit decals provided nothing to this particular model so I really can't comment on their performance but they look very nice on the sheet. They have perfect printing and register with bright colours and a full set of stencils. The AeroMaster decals worked pretty well, though. You get the individual markings for all four versions on this sheet, as well as enough national markings and stencils for two full builds, so it's really good value for

money. They settle down quite well with setting solutions and really bring the kit to life.

Final Details

Once this lot are dry it's time to get things finished and there's an awful lot left still to do. Basically there are so many little bits left it takes nearly as long to finish it as it did to do the rest. Of particular note are the multi-part canopy and the dreadfully shaped propeller blades. Not sure what's going on with them but the profile of the blade is just way off the mark, although they do have the correct handed ones for left and right engines. Before the canopy is fitted the whole kit gets a good spray of Xtracolor XDFF Flat Varnish to dull it all down and the masking is removed from the camera bays and landing light. This leaves the task of fitting the canopy in the open position and remembering that the side panels are wind-down window affairs, they have to be cut and trimmed to fit. The red 'NO STEP' decals look nice here to accentuate the slightly odd arrangement with the main section hinged back over the nacelle; it's a pretty distinctive look. The final steps are the aerial leads made from fishing line and getting the exhaust staining right on the tail booms. For the Lead Oxide residue Tamiya XF-55 Deck Tan looks pretty good. Thinned out with Mr Color Levelling Thinner and sprayed at high pressure (20psi) it atomises into a very fine mist, allowing the layers to be built up slowly, so you can make it as fine or as filthy as you like. I went for filthy, of course!

Verdict

The P-38, in all its versions, is a stunning machine and this kit captures its look very nicely. It has some problems around the lack of detail in certain areas and you'll need that filler, but all in all it's pretty good. This particular box, with the four versions on offer, is an excellent addition to the Academy range of Lightnings and is well worth the money and the effort needed to get the best out of it.

Me 262B-1a

1/48th

by Steve A. Evans

The Messerschmitt Me 262 is nothing short of legendary. As Germany's first jet fighter of the War it will always have a huge place in the history books but it's got to be its looks that really fascinate. It's an airborne shark, nothing less than a menacing shape however you look at it. The two-seat variants are a bit clumsier looking, with a hump-backed grace all of their own but most of us still like them. So I was very happy to see this particular release from HobbyBoss in their line-up of this aircraft. They've already done just about every single-seat version, so this was the next logical step. They also made an excellent decision to do the twin-seat trainer first as this is a rarity in the model world. Well, it's still a rarity because I am massively annoyed to tell you that it is impossible to make a standard Me 262B-1a trainer from the plastic bits in the box. The only variant that you can do is the common night-fighter B-1a/U1. I hate it when a kit manufacturer markets a kit as something it's not. I also hate starting a kit when I'm grumpy with it, as this usually sets the mood for the whole build.

So, after the cursing and swearing never to buy a HobbyBoss kit again, I eventually calmed down enough to start the build and this is actually a fine bit of plastic moulding. You get nine sprues of medium grey-coloured plastic and it's well up to the HobbyBoss standard these days. The details are both finely done and sharply moulded. The exterior is devoid of any overdone rivet detail, with good recessed panels and lovely shapes. There is only the tiniest bits of flash apparent on some of the smaller parts and with the inclusion of a lot of interior detail there's plenty going on in there. The decals in the box, although totally pointless, are very well printed, with lots of stencils included plus the instrument panels. The swastikas are split of course but everything else looks good and you know that

Technical Data
HobbyBoss 1/48th Messerschmitt Me 262B-1a
Kit No.: 80378
Material: IM
UK Importer: Creative Models Ltd
UK Price: £16.99

The box top art is atmospheric, if a bit crude. The contents are beautiful looking plastic, as usual, and also completely erroneous because you cannot build a 'B-1a' from the bits in the box!

The cockpit detailing is very good. The crisp mouldings make painting easier but you will definitely need a set of seat belts

nosewheel assembly to chose from and with the radio gear, oxygen bottles and compass in the rear, it's looking pretty full in there. You also need to stuff about 10g of weight in the nose as well, so it's a good job there are plenty of cubby-holes to hide it away in. There is also a nose weight supplied in the kit as a metal version of part M1, but it's not mentioned at all in the instructions, which is a bit odd. The fuselage halves need the joint line lightly sanded to remove a few mould irregularities but after that the centre-line is all but invisible. The joints on the engine nacelles, however, need a little bit of love and attention because both the front nose cones and rear jet pipe sections don't quite line up with the rest. It's the same story for the nacelle-to-wing fit and the wing-to-fuselage joint as well. Super-glue comes in handy for a fill and glue session but of course this also means there are sanding and scribing sessions to follow. There is more of the same along the joints in the nose, around the gun bay, as the doors are moulded to be open. None of this was helped by using the replacement metal nose weight, which seems cruder than its plastic counterpart, so there's a little bit of misalignment

they are going to perform superbly, because they always do from this kit maker.

Construction is taken care of in just seven stages in the well-drawn instructions, beginning with that interior. It may be nicely done but it's the cockpit that's the culprit in the wrong variant saga. The rear seat and bulkhead should be much further back, with a repeater instrument panel for the instructor pilot, as well as full flight and engine controls of course. Instead, all you're given is the short tub and radar gear of the nightfighter version. No doubt the aftermarket resin correction sets will be available by the time you read this and HobbyBoss will have released the nightfighter variant in another box, but I'm still grumpy at this moment in time. You get some fine looking detailing for the cockpit, complete with the decals for the main instrument panel if you want and it's all easy to build and paint. You get a full gun-bay to play with as well, with MK 108 30mm cannon on show, along with the ammunition chutes. There are two types of

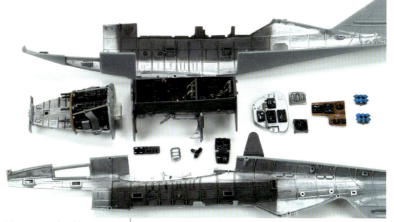

That great looking interior continues on into the rear fuselage, although 90% of that is going to remain hidden

of the parts. I chucked the masked-off canopies onto the kit with some PVA to temporarily hold them in place and it was time for paint.

Colour

Ignoring the fact that the painting guide is useless (yes, still grumpy) I turned to my reference material for inspiration and thankfully any of the Me 262 nightfighter versions look utterly splendid. I'd already done the 1/32nd Trumpeter version for Airframe and Miniature No.1, so I needed something just a little different. This

The engine nacelles are simple, yet effective but careful aligning of the parts is necessary

The fit of the completed nacelle to the wing is OK, not brilliant but at least they have remembered the footstep on the top of the left one

The joints are all a bit troublesome in this one, possibly as much my fault as the kits as I was doing it between more interesting projects

The nose doors are moulded to be open, so a little sliver of plasticard is needed to take up the slack

The transparencies are always good in HobbyBoss kits and this one is no exception

The primer gets the plastic ready for the paint job, as well as highlighting all the bits not yet smoothed out

Black underside is actually Tamiya XF-85 Rubber Black and don't worry, the lighter grey panels will fade in once weathered and oversprayed

This is a lot of fiddly stuff, not forgetting there are also the aerial wires and cockpit canopies to sort as well

came in the form of RLM 82 upper surfaces for the wings and tail, while the mottled RLM 76 fuselage had an overspray of RLM 02. Coupled with the dark markings this makes a very sombre looking machine, a little bit sinister from some angles, which is rather nice. It doesn't really mat-

The RLM 82 wings and tail with panel lines accentuated with a slightly darkened shade

ter which order you decide to paint this kind of thing because whichever way you do it, masking will be involved. I opted for the black bits first, then the green, then the mottled fuselage and it all worked out OK. No pre-shading involved, as I seem to have fallen out of love with that technique, all the panels and fading were done with post-shading of darker paint tones and pastel dust, not to mention the infinitely useful Tamiya X-19 Smoke. Paint chips were courtesy of my Pentel soft lead silver pencil and with some

The fuselage RLM 76 gets mottled and oversprayed with RLM 02 to tone it down, giving the whole thing a rather sombre look

Johnson's Klear over the top of it all it was time for the decals.

As mentioned, the markings are incorrect for the nightfighter version so a quick trawl through the spares box came up with some suitable ones. These aircraft had only the basic stuff on them anyway so it was just a case of finding the right swastikas, W/Nr. and fuselage crosses, everything else came from the kit sheet. As I suspected, the HobbyBoss decals worked beautifully and with the carrier film scrubbed away they look stunning. Sealed in with some more Klear it was ready for a thin oil wash (502 Abteilung Abt110 Black) and it was on with the final bits.

Final Details

What a stash of bits is still left to do, and it's all the delicate stuff as well. It's all aerials, wires and doors but the main points are the excellent and sturdy fit of the undercarriage units, the drop tanks under the nose and the slightly clumsy looking antenna on the FuG 218 Neptun V radar. These Stag antlers really need replacing with something a lot finer but I've left it all alone for now just to show you what the kit items look like.

The final surface finish is Xtracolor XDFF flat

varnish and then it's time to tackle the canopies. Both front and back items need some attention before they get glued into position. The obvious things missing are the locking levers and the grab handles, made from stretched sprue, and the retention wires and springs, made from fishing line and fine wire respectively. The front canopy also needs a missing frame put in, but don't forget it's internal only, so it has to be painted on from the inside, or very thin stretched sprue would do a fine job. After that the canopies are stuck down with odourless superglue and I'm calling this one complete.

Verdict

Yes, I know, I'm still grumpy so this might not be too complimentary but apart from the utter and total failure of HobbyBoss to give us the kit it says on the box, it's actually really nice. The plastic is excellent and the build process, although not as faultless as some of their other kits, is still pretty easy. Accuracy looks to be pretty good with no major flaws and it certainly has the correct 'sit' on its sturdy undercarriage. The decals are good and you can make a fine looking Nachtjäger, but don't forget, that's all you can make!

✠ **Messerschmitt Bf 109G-10/U4, 'Black 2', of the Kroat Jagdstaffel, Eichwalde, November 1944**
RLM 74/75/76 scheme with RLM 04 (Gelb) nose and fuselage band, rudder, and underside of wingtips

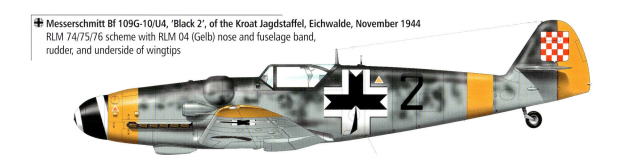

✠ **Messerschmitt Bf 109G-10/AS, 'Yellow 8' flown by Maresciallo Attilio Sanson, 5a Squadriglia II° Gruppo Caccia, Aviazione Nazionale Repubblicana, Osoppo, March 1945**
RLM 74/75/76 finish with black/white spinner; standard German markings in usual positions; yellow '8' on fuselage sides; Italian flags, fringed in yellow, on fuselage sides and fin. 'Diavolo Rosso' emblem on nose (both sides)

✠ **Messerschmitt Bf 109G-10 (ex-Bulgarian Air Force), W/Nr.610937, 9644, 'White 44', Yugoslav Air Force, spring 1945**
Medium grey/dark brown upper surfaces with light blue undersides; national markings in six positions; black serial on fin, white code on fuselage sides

✠ **Fiat G.55 Centauro Serie I, 'Black 7' flown by Capitano Ugo Drago, 1^ Squadriglia, 2° Gruppo Caccia Aviazione Nazionale Repubblicana, Cascina Vega, May 1944**
Sand/brown/green upper surfaces with Grigio Azzuro Chiaro undersides; yellow underside of engine cowling; spinner has white quarter; black '7' outlined in white on fuselage sides; unit badge in white on nose

✠ **Focke-Wulf Fw 190A-8, 'Black 8', IV (Strum) JG.3 'Udet', June 1944**
RLM 74/75/76 finish with mottling in RLM 74/75 and possibly RLM 02 on fuselage sides. black nose section with section on fuselage having a red outline; black '8' outlined in white and variant of III Gruppe wavy identity marking on white fuselage band; yellow/red spinner; unit badge on nose

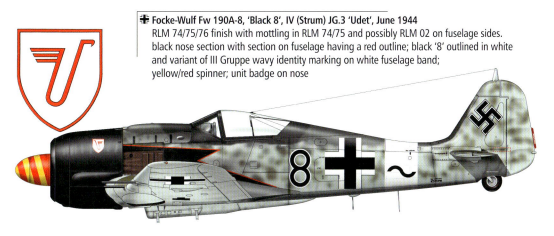

✠ **Focke-Wulf Fw 190D, W/Nr.600424, 'Red 1', flown by Lt Heinz 'Heino Sachsenberg,**
Staffelkapitän Platzchutzstaffel JV44, München-Riem, April 1945
RLM 82/83 upper surfaces with fuselage sides and vertical tail surfaces in RLM 76 with mottling in the
top colours; RLM 23 Rot undersides with thin white bands; yellow/RLM 70 spinner;
pilot's slogan in white; red '1', thinly outlined in white

✠ **Focke-Wulf Fw 190D-9, W/Nr.500658, 'Black 12', III./KG(J)27**
RLM 82/75/76 finish with black spinner and white spiral; RLM 25 Hellgrün/RLM 21 white
checks on rear fuselage; all markings and '12' on fuselage in black

✠ **Fiat G.55 Serie I, S/No.MM.91147, 'Blue 21', 3^ Squadriglia, 1° Gruppo Caccia 'Bonet',**
Aviazione Nazionale Repubblicana, July 1944
Nocciola Chiaro/Verde Oliva Scuro upper surfaces in a 'herringbone' pattern, with Grigio Azzurro
Chiaro undersides; standard national markings; light blue/white codes,
light blue/yellow serial; light blue lettering on fin; white spinner with
black backplate and spiral; white 'Bonet' motif above codes

✠ **Heinkel He 162A-2, W/Nr.310018, 'White 5', I./JG 1, flown by Staffelkapitän Hptm Helmut Könnecke, Leck, May 1945**
RLM 81/82/65 finish with RLM 23 Rot air intake and arrow on nose; white '5' thinly outlined in black; all other markings in
black only

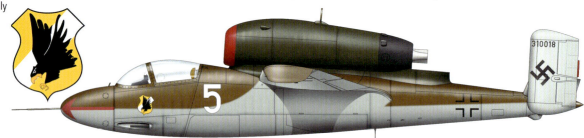

✠ **Heinkel He 162A-2, W/Nr.120021, 'Yellow 3', II./JG 1, Leck, May 1945**
RLM 81/82/65 scheme; wing crosses in black only; '3' on fuselage sides and air intakes in RLM 04 Gelb

✠ **Macchi C.205V Veltro Serie I (with Serie III wings), S/No.M.M.9350, 1-3, 3^ Squadriglia (Ariete), 1º Gruppo ANR, Friuli, April 1944**
RLM 74/75 uppersurfaces with RLM 76 undersides; Giallo Cromo underside of engine cowling; white rear fuselage band; white rear fuselage band; codes in blue/white; unit badge on nose; '3' in black over a red/white/green pennant on mainwheel doors

✠ **Messerschmitt Me 262A-1a, W/Nr.500042, B3+AA, flown by Obslt. V. Riesedel Freiherr zu Eisenback, Geschwaderkommodore KG(J) 54, Gibelstadt, February 1945**
RLM 81/82/76 with codes in black and individual letter in blue; blue nose cone with white outline

✠ **Messerschmitt Me 163B, 'White 42' (probably V22, W/Nr.310051), training Gruppe III./JG400 (13 or 14 Staffel)**
The aircraft is RLM 02 overall with RLM 80/81 mottling on the fuselage sides and tail and the same bands of the same colours above the wings; black/white markings on fuselage, white-only crosses above wings, black-only crosses under the wings; RLM 21 (white) '42' on fin and rudder; nose cone is red with a thin white outline

✠ **Messerschmitt Me 262A-1a, 'Green 1', flown by Maj. Rudolf Sinner, Gruppenkommandeur III./JG 7, Brandenburg-Briest, March 1945**
RLM 81/82/76 finish with green '1' under unit crest outlined in white; Kommandeur's double chevron in black and white; III Gruppe vertical bar in white over red/blue band around rear fuselage; armed with a pair of W/Gr.21 rocket launchers

✠ **Focke-Wulf Ta 152H-1, (W/Nr. unknown), 'Green 8', Stab./JG 301, April 1945**
RLM 81/82 upper surfaces with RLM 76 undersides; yellow/red rear fuselage bands; green '8', outlined in black, on fuselage sides; horizontal green band over the fuselage bands; white spiral on spinner

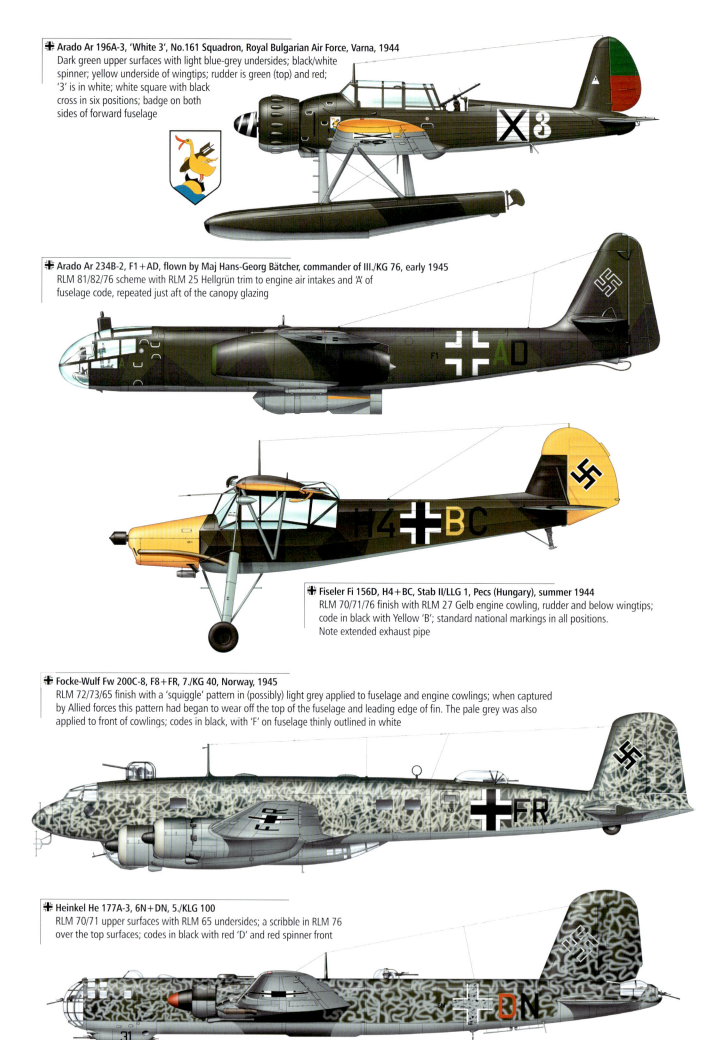

✠ **Heinkel He 219A-2, W/Nr.290126, D5+BL, 3./NJG 3**
RLM 22 (Black) on all undersides; top surfaces in RLM 75/76; all markings in white, except 'BL' of code, which is probably in RLM 77 (some sources quote RLM 04 Gelb); cowlings are RLM 75, spinner is black/white. Note 'VI' in black below windscreen

✠ **Junkers Ju 87D-5, 'White 13', 1/2 Orljak, Royal Bulgarian Air Force, summer 1944**
RLM 70/71 upper surfaces with RLM 65 undersides; yellow underside of wingtips and fuselage band; national markings in six positions; '13' in white; rudder in green and red; red/white spiral on spinner

✠ **Junkers Ju 87G-2, W/Nr.494193, flown by Oblt Hans Rudel, Stab/SG 2, Seregélyes (Central Hungary), late 1944**
RLM 70/71 upper surfaces with RLM 65 undersides; RLM 27 Gelb rear fuselage band, underside of wingtips and 'V' below port wing; national markings in white only on top colours; black/white spiral on spinner; chevron and bar markings in black, outlined in white. Note the misalignment of the W/Nr. on the port side of the fin

✠ **Junkers Ju 88A-4, '137', flown by Captain. av. Eusebie Popovici, No.5 Bomber Wing of the Royal Rumanian Air Force, 1st Air Corps, summer 1944**
Standard Luftwaffe 70/71/65 scheme with yellow underside wingtips, spinners and rear fuselage band; national markings in six positions; tri-colour flash on top of rudder

✠ **Junkers Ju 188A-3, G2+BR, z.KG 26, Norway, 1945**
RLM 70/71 on upper surfaces covered in RLM 76 squiggle (except on engine cowlings); undersides in RLM 65. codes in black except for 'B', which is in yellow outline; national markings in white on upper surfaces

P-47D Thunderbolt

1/32nd
by Dani Zamarbide

All those who love combat aviation will be familiar of one of the classics of World War II, the Republic P-47 Thunderbolt. I will not describe the history of this aircraft in general, instead I will focus on the model I've done for this special, which is the well-known 'bubbletop' version. Initially these machines came to Europe with the standard USAAF scheme of Olive Drab over Neutral Grey, but once the Allies gained air superiority this scheme gave way to natural metal overall. Although the type basically carried these two schemes, during the final months of the war, especially when they began to fly over the skies of Nazi Germany, many USAAF units adopted camouflage of greens and greys similar to the RAF shades since the Thunderbolts were operating from bases in the UK. For this reason these colours also adopted almost unique patterns composing large patches or mottling of lighter colours over the others; quite unique. The real controversy with these aircraft though, which can't be seen in period photographs, is the underside. Many modellers have painted this in the standard Neutral Grey but I have opted for natural metal. My reasoning is that these planes were, by this stage of the war, natural metal overall and so the camouflage, once applied, was done with RAF colours over the the top, thus leaving the underside in natural metal because they would not have repainted it in the (older) Neutral Grey? Curiously, I will say that with this particular aircraft that I am depicting, there are several colour photos that some may claim show another potential scheme altogether, but I am going with the combination of colours listed above.

Construction

Hasegawa's kit is simply very good, and in my eyes it would be perfect if it had rivet details, other than that, it is superb. When I

page 72 ▶

Technical Data
Hasegawa 1/32nd Republic P-47D Thunderbolt 'Bubbletop'
Kit No.: ST27 (#08077)
Material: IM
UK Importer: Ripmax Ltd
UK Price: OOP

Engine

The spark plugs are drilled out so that ignition wires could be added later

The overall colour applied is White Aluminium

The cylinder detail is picked out with Tamiya X-19 Smoke

The remainder of the detail is picked out using AK Interactive Dark Brown Wash

The reduction casing is sprayed XF-53 (Neutral Grey)

Shadows are added with a fine pencil

Paint chipping is done with Vallejo Sky Grey

The distributor is picked out in black

A random number is hand-painted on the side in white, to add a bit of interest

With the cables picked out in a tan colour, the bolt heads are now picked out in silver

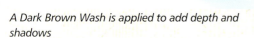

The whole unit gets a coat of matt varnish

A Dark Brown Wash is applied to add depth and shadows

The front engine ring is painted white aluminium, the bolts receive a Dark Brown Wash and is attached to the engine

A similar series of highlight colours and dark washes are applied to the rest of the engine, which gets a coat of matt varnish

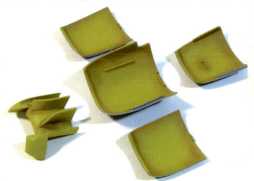

The engine cowlings are painted with XF-4, with some darker areas to give tonal contrast

The completed engine in its cowling, note the paint chips done with a light yellowish colour along the edge of the intake splitter

Cockpit

The pilot figure in the kit is superb, only needing the oxygen pipe made from coiled wire and the belts (with RB Productions excellent etched buckles) and other details made from lead sheet

Before the interior is painted, it is first test-fitted into the fuselage halves, to ensure everything fits

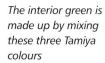 

The interior green is made up by mixing these three Tamiya colours

Everything is coated with the green, and sealed with acrylic gloss varnish

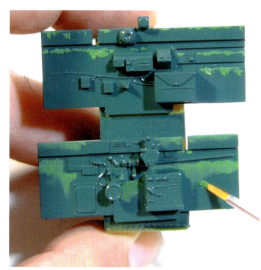

Highlights are added to the whole of the cockpit using various shades of oil paint, which is blended in with thinner; the sidewalls are shown here

Here Ochre oil paint is used along the bottom edges to create the dirt and mud in this area…

…which is blended in

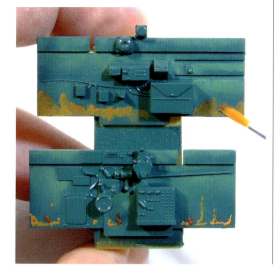

Scratches are applied with a toothpick; the 'mud' is clumped using Humbrol enamel thinners

The floor of the cockpit has received the same lightening effect, then the pilot's face is carefully hand-painted…

…followed by the painting of his helmet, flying jacket and seat belts…

…and finally his trousers

The completed figure once the overall varnish coat is applied and the face has received the Skin Tone Glaze from the AZ Interactive range

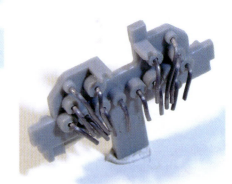

The side consoles have the various boxes picked out in black…

…followed by various details picked out in silver…

The back of the instrument panel has solder added to each instrument…

…and finally all the other details picked out in various colours before each unit received a coat of varnish

In situ within the starboard fuselage half

The instrument panel received a coat of black, followed by the instrument dial pointers etc. being picked out in white…

…other details are picked out in grey…

…and yet more details are picked out…

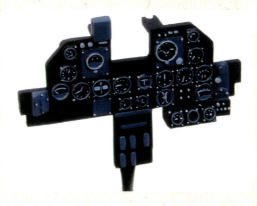

…followed by a bit of colour to liven things up…

…the completed instrument panel with the rudder pedals added, suitably 'muddy' using pastels and fixer

The gunsight has the two pads added to the front from plasticard and is carefully painted and highlighted

The gunsight attached to the front bulkhead; note the 'dirt' added to the bottom of the bulkhead as it is behind the equally muddy rudder pedals

All the various components of the cockpit interior laid out

Undercarriage

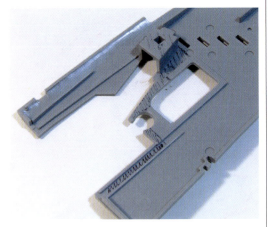

The kit undercarriage bays are replaced with the resin set from Aires (#2122), so the corresponding areas had to be cut away from the kit parts

The difference in the kit parts (top) in comparison with the Aires versions (bottom) is self evident

The base colour is Tamiya XF-4

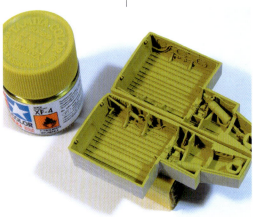

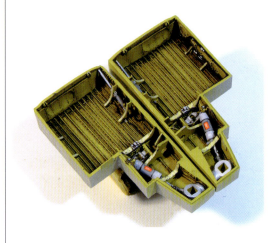

With the area sealed with gloss, the various details can be picked out with grey, black etc.

◀ page 66 start any build of a type with a radial engine, I always begin the assembly with the engine, mainly because it is one of the more tedious tasks. The engine in this kit, as supplied, is perfectly adequate if you're going to leave it with the engine cowls on. The detail is very good and it only needs the wiring to each of its cylinders with 0.5mm solder. You need to add this because once the engine is placed inside the cowls, the entire front view is more realistic once the model is completed. All the interior of the cowls are in the typical greenish-yellow (Yellow Zinc Chromate) colour used by American equipment and for which I find Tamiya XF-4 to be perfect. As for the engine cylinders, these are painted with X-11 from the Tamiya enamel range of paints and the front gearbox is picked out in a neutral grey, followed by a dark brown colour from the Vallejo range for the cables. To age the somewhat bright nature of the overall silver colour I applied a wash of AK Interactive dark brown, then used various oil paints to add light and dark to replicate dirt etc. on other parts of the motor. The entire engine assembly is made ready for the subsequent final assembly of the model by making it into a sub-assembly complete with the cowlings. It is in this part that the model, in my opinion, fails a bit because the cowling does not come in one piece as seen in other Hasegawa models. Instead it has the four elements of the unit, which is great if you want to leave these open to expose the engine and

Paint chips are replicated with dark grey paint, and a dark wash is applied before each is sealed with matt varnish

although the fit of the four parts is very good, it always involves more work than necessary, and you have to ensure that the overall shape of the cowling remains symmetrical.

Once I had done the engine, I turned my attention to the cockpit interior. Again Hasegawa gives us a sensational cockpit and above all, something that I like, a figure with spectacular quality that in many ways exceeds even some resin figures in the scale. So to start, once I have glued together the pieces that make up the body, I attach him to the seat and once placed, I add seat belts made from photo-etched buckles and tin foil and attach these to the seat. Once finished, I always apply a grey primer then set about painting the figure with various colours from the Vallejo range. To continue with the rest of the cockpit, I make a mix using page 78 ▶

Propeller

The basic colours are applied to the blades and hub

Paint chips are first done with a silver watercolour pencil

With the stencil decals applied and an overall coat of acrylic gloss varnish applied (and dried), dabs of medium grey oil paint are applied to the leading edge of each blade

Ochre oil paint is applied around the tips

The oil is blended together with thinners…

…this is continued, drawing the oil paint across the blade in the direction of the airflow when the propeller is turning, thinning the layer more and more until it is a very fine layer

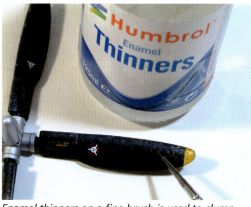

Enamel thinners on a fine brush is used to clump the underlaying oil more and intensify the colour

The end result

Main Wheels

The kit wheel (right), as you can see, is far less detailed than the resin example from BarracudaCast (#BR32060) on the left

The hub is painted aluminium and the tyre painted black

Dark Sea Grey from Vallejo is used to highlight the tread pattern

The whole thing is given an overall coat of acrylic gloss varnish

First thin lines of medium grey oil paint are applied...

...followed by similar lines of Ochre...

...then with thinners they are blended together, but still confined to the outer edge of the tyre

Three earth tones from the AK Interactive pigments range are used to create the 'dirt' in the treads

The recessed detail of the hub received a dark wash from the AK Interactive Paneliner range

The completed wheels once a coat of matt varnish is applied

Drop Tank

The overall scheme is the same silver as the airframe; the gunmetal is applied in this tapering pattern, and whilst still wet is dabbed with a brush to create these marks

The upper surface only has the effect around the filler at the front, as well as some darkening around the centre feed-in

Some very dark grey oil paint is dabbed on…

…followed by more of the Ochre…

…and it is all blended together with thinner…

…before more thinner is used to create these irregular marks in the overall filter layer

Spilt fuel from the filler is created with 'Kerosene Leaks & Stains' from AK Interactive

Followed by 'Wash: Engine & Turbines', also from AK

And finally ''Aircraft Engine Oil' from AK

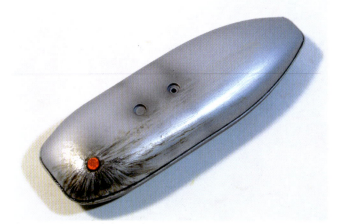

The completed tank from above…

…and below

Guns

The kit gun barrels are replaced with the superb brass ones from Master Model (#AM-32-004)

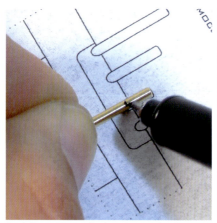

Each barrel is marked, using scale plans, so that you know how far in they have to be placed into the wing

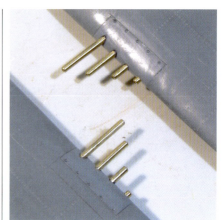

The end result is most impressive and vastly superior to the kit parts

Wing Root

Some filler is required at the wing root, although Mr Surfacer is sufficient

Embossing tape (Dymo etc.) is used to form a flexible ruler, so that the panel lines can be scribed back in

Using the 0.75mm wheel on the 'Rosie the Riveter' tool, the rivets are added

Paint – Overall

The airframe is masked ready for the painting to begin…

…and this includes the underside

The rudder is first painted white…

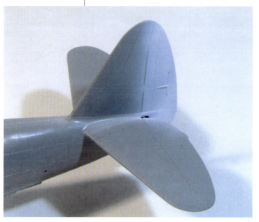

…and the red…

...and once dry it is masked off

The windscreen is sprayed black, so that this shows through inside instead of the outer silver colour

The undersides are sprayed with silver from the Tamiya enamel paint range

The upper camouflage is marked out lightly in pencil, and the first colour to go on is Ocean Grey (XF-82)...

The exhaust outlets and turbo-supercharger exhaust are masked and sprayed with Gunmetal from the same paint range

...followed by Dark Green (XF-81)

The completed basic overall colours

Paint – Markings

The first task as far as painting the maskings is concerned, is to mask off the red tip of the cowling …

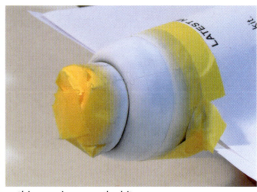

…this area is sprayed white…

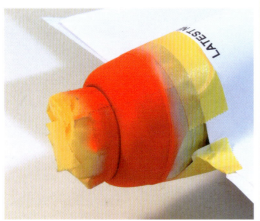

…the red is applied

The masking is now removed from both the nose and tail

◀ *page 72* Tamiya paints for dull (dark) Chromate Green using the following ratio:
- XF-70 (45%)
- X-14 (45%)
- XF-1 (10%)

To this mix I add a little X-20 solvent to thin the paint so it can be applied with an airbrush all around the inside of the cockpit area. Then, following images of a real cockpit (if possible, in colour), with various colours I detail paint both the instrument panel and the rest of the cockpit. With respect to the instrument panel I have to say that I have added all the wiring at the back of the instruments, just for added realism and interest. With all the cockpit interior painting finished that whole assembly is built up as a tub that that subsequently, before closing the fuselage halves, will be placed inside.

My attention now turns to the exterior of the airframe, so I start this with adding all the missing rivet detail. You need a good set of scale plans, which show the rivet locations and once you have that, it is simply a case of transferring these lines of rivets to each of the areas of the model, marking their locations with a pencil. Once I have all the lines of rivets marked, with a special tool, in my case 'Rosie the Riveter' fitted with a wheel suitable for 1/32nd scale, I systematically apply all the rivets. For this phase, I recommend doing it in stages, as it is very tedious, but once completed, it will bring more realism to the model without any doubt.

The next areas to receive attention are the undercarriage bays. As depicted in the kit these are very simple, so they are improved using the resin upgrade set from Aires that is specifically designed for this model. Following the instructions the fit of these new resin wells is perfect, although I do recommend you paint them before securing them within the wings.

Now with the engine inside its cowlings, the new wheel wells added and cockpit detailed and fitted into the fuselage, the general assembly of the model can be undertaken. The fit is simply spectacular, although it requires a little care, especially with the wing-to-fuselage joint. After the final assembly I checked everything carefully to see if any areas required filler and/or sanding, then I masked off the cockpit, wheel wells and engine cowl front so that I could start the painting phase.

Colour

To begin the painting phase, I start with the lightest colour, and in this case that is the natural metal. To replicate this I use the silver from the Tamiya enamel paint range (X-11). To give different shades, I just add a few drops of a dark metallic colour such as Gunmetal from the same manufacturer, as they mix easily. After applying the colour, along the underside with a pencil I draw the contours of the camouflage demarcation and the pattern on the upper surfaces for the areas of green and grey. Once the *page 84* ▶

The white and black stripes on the underside of the wing and fuselage are masked, with the white being the first colour to be applied…

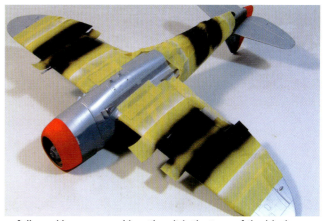

…followed by more masking, then it is the turn of the black…

…the completed stripes

Montex masks are used to apply all the national markings, so once each outer element of each mask in position, it is time to apply the white

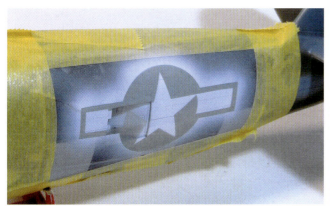

…now position the inner masks, so that everything is lined up…

…followed by the outer sections, which may seem mad, but now…

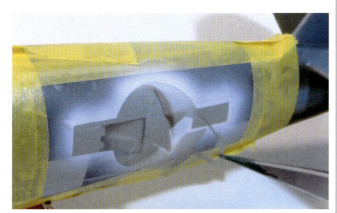

…you can peel back the masks for those areas that are to be sprayed blue, knowing that everything fits and the stars and bars white elements are in the correct position/alignment

The blue of the insigina can be applied

Masks are fiddly, but well worth the effort because the markings now are truly 'sprayed on'

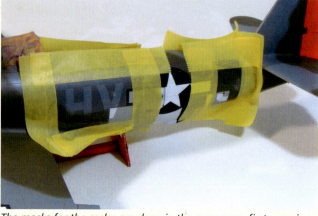

The masks for the codes are done in the same way, first ensuring they are correctly positioned…

…then applying white, followed by putting the inner elements of each mask in place…

…then take out the central bits to just leave the outer edge masks in place…

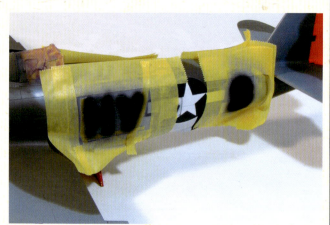

…then apply the black

The end result is very effective

The serial numbers on the tail are done in the same way

As are the stars 'n' bars on the underside; note this machine has them under both wings, not just the starboard as is usually the case

Paint – Nose Art

The Montex masks include the nose art as a decal, but this is just used as the basis to sketch the outline out on the nose in pencil

Each colour is put down, one at a time, starting with the dark blue…

…the light blue…

…the yellow…

…the midnight blue…

…the brown…

…the white…

…the white text…

…and finally the black outline, this time using a draughtsman's pen and ink

The completed nose art

Weathering

Paint chips had to be painted on using grey, green or orange, depending on the area being treated

The panel lines on the red areas are picked out with a pencil, while those on the rest of the airframe are done with a draughtsman's pen

White, grey and blue watercolour pencils are used to create more chipping, which you can see extends to the areas on the inboard upper wing panels as well

The overall chipping effects achieved with paint and watercolour pencils

The model is now sealed with acrylic gloss varnish

Paneliner for brown and green camouflage from AK Interactive is applied to all the recessed detail…

…the excess is removed with a clean cloth

A special mix to reproduce 'black oil' is applied to all the access panels etc., with the excess removed with a cloth and thinners

Dots of Yellow Ochre oil paint are applied to create highlights, and blended in with thinner

The same process is done with the inboard section of the wing, but only on areas of green paint

This is blended in with a wide brush and thinners

The effect is done on all the green areas, but much less the further out on the wings, or down the fuselage you go

Using light grey oil paint, the same method is applied to all the Ocean Grey areas

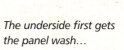

The underside first gets the panel wash…

…the exhaust stains are added around the main exhaust and supercharger outlets…

…this staining is put on in a heavier layer from the exhausts back along the underside of the fuselage, back from each gun ejector port and aft of each main wheel well

The undercarriage doors have to receive similar weathering effects as the underside of the fuselage

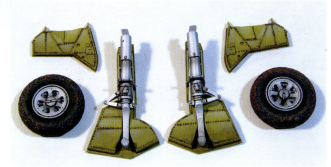

The inside of the undercarriage doors have the same painting effects used for the interior of the wheel wells

◀ *page 78* basic colours are on I can then start painting the squadron bands, such as the red one around the nose. After this comes a slightly complicated and tedious stage because I used Montex masks for all the markings. What you need to keep in mind when using such masks is that the American stars have to be correctly orientated and the letters of the fuselage code are black, trimmed in white. Once I was done with all the masks, it was time to apply the nose art and although this is supplied as a decal by Montex I decided, with reference to the dimensions of the decal, to hand-draw the marking myself and then colour it in using suitable colours from the Vallejo acrylic paint range.

Now I start the process of ageing and to do this I used a very light grey, again from Vallejo, applied with a fine brush. I apply small paint chips using this colour to all the Ocean Grey areas, especially in those areas that received the most wear, such as the engine cowling, wing root and around the cockpit. Repeat the same procedure with a sandy yellow for the green areas and finally, with an ochre colour, any red areas. The next step is to seal the whole paint scheme thus far with a layer of gloss varnish and once this is fully dry, to apply a panel wash from the AK-Interactive Paneliner series. This is applied to all the panel lines and the rivets and, once dry, the excess is removed with a solvent impregnated cloth.

To finish the weathering process, I apply oil paints of various colours to create areas of light and dark on each of the panels to further accentuate, and give greater presence to the colours by breaking them up once this stage is completed. Finally, a layer of matt varnish is applied to seal everything in.

Final Details

I conclude the building with exterior parts such as wheels, which in this case I replaced the kit parts with the resin examples from Barracuda

All the various bits and pieces laid out prior to final assembly

Studios, which are of excellent quality. The plastic machine gun barrels in the kit were replaced with the superb metal examples manufactured by Master Models of Poland. I also built, painted and weathered the undercarriage legs and doors, propeller, canopy and the fuel tank. Do take care with the propeller though, as Hasegawa offer four different types of propeller suitable for the P-47, so you will need to study period images and determine which of them you need for the particular aircraft you are depicting. Once all of these parts are ready it only remains to place them, add smaller parts like the tip lights etc., and then replicate the staining around the gun ports and the exhausts.

Verdict

My experience in building this kit was such that I am completely satisfied with the model Hasegawa have produced. The type has countless options for colour schemes and variants, so it will not be in the too distant future that I repeat the experience with this kit. In my opinion it is a simple kit of great quality and details, with excellent fit of parts, which is done to a scale that once it is built results in a spectacular looking model.

Highly recommended to all, as are all the other subjects in this series from Hasegawa.

Spitfire PR Mk XIX

The Spitfire PR Mk XIX entered service in June 1944. There were two variants built and the easiest way to tell one from the other is that the earlier version has the drop down cockpit door. The type also had the distinction of carrying out the last operational RAF Spitfire flight in April 1954. In my opinion the combination of the long Griffon engine and clean airframe makes the PR Mk XIX one of the most beautiful aeroplanes you will ever see fly. In comparison to their fighter brothers the photo-reconnaissance versions haven't proved as popular amongst kit manufacturers, especially in my preferred scale of 1/32nd. The only Griffon Spitfires produced so far are the classic Matchbox (now Revell) Mk 22/24 and the Pacific Coast Mk XIV. The other option you have is to go with the resin conversion offered by Grey Matter used in conjunction with one of the many issues of the Mk V by Hasegawa. The Pacific Coast kit hadn't been released when I built this one so that was the route I took. I also needed

Technical Data	
Hasegawa 1/32nd Spitfire Mk Vb + Grey Matters resin conversion set	
Kit No.:	#S18 (#ST2 or ST2X)
Material:	IM, R, VF
UK Importer:	Ripmax Ltd (Hasegawa)
UK Price:	£OOP

1/32nd

by Alan Bottoms

Note: As Libor has shown you how to build the PR Mk XIX in 1/72nd and Airfix do an excellent version in 1/48th, we thought you might like to see one in 1/32nd, made with the help of an aftermarket conversion set.

to add a late-war Sutton harness set by Eduard and a fair bit of traditional modelling before I could sit back and admire the graceful lines. The Hasegawa kit is quite old so raised panel lines are the order of the day but this isn't as much of a problem as you'd think because with a PR version you are removing detail rather than adding it to the wings. There is no armament fitted, the wing being full of fuel. The conversion set is dominated by the replacement Griffon engine and five-blade propeller but does also include the carburettor intake, two large underwing radiators, elevators, tail and main wheels and a vacform canopy. Unfortunately the canopy is the only part specific to a PR Mk XIX variant so some scratch-building is needed if you want to do any of the internal camera bay. The other problem of course is decals, in particular the roundels because these were smaller than the equivalent fighters of the time, so I needed to raid the spares box. Armed with a large pile of reference books, the main one being The Aviation Workshop On Target Profile No.8 Photo Reconnaissance Spitfires, I could start building.

Construction

I began my build with the wings. The first job was to cut the cannon bulges off with a photo-etch razor saw. This left a hole in the top of each wing so the bulges I had removed were used as plugs fixed (turned upside down and reinserted) into place with some cyanoacrylate and activator.

The upper wing can now be filled and sanded with just a touch of Mr Surfacer to finish off. It was time to scribe some panel lines now. These were drawn on with a pencil then scribed using an Olfa P-Cutter and a straight edge. Moving to the underside the single radiator and oil cooler were removed and the openings filled with plasticard ready for the new resin radiators. As with the top surface the gun bulges and cartridge ejection slots have to be deleted before scribing the new panel lines. Moving onto the tailplanes and elevators a set of resin extended mass balance elevators are provided. The old ones were cut off and the tips of the tailplanes cut back ready for the new ones. With the bulk of the work on the flying surfaces finished it was time to start looking at the fuselage. There is a lot of surgery here so it's worth spending some time to study the conversion instructions and scale plans before you start cutting. It would be difficult to get the cuts accurate with the fuselage halves separated so the cuts were made leaving a little extra material to adjust for fit later. The cockpit was built up pretty much as it came in the kit although there are a few little touches that will make a difference to the look of the finished article. The first of these was to drill out the lightening holes in the frames. The handgrip on the control column was wrapped with thin solder to

beef it up a little and the moulded crowbar was replaced with a new one made from plastic rod. I added the leather back pad to the seat using a piece of wine bottle foil. It was cut to shape and the ribs embossed with a pin and a straight edge. Once the interior was painted the pre-painted Eduard harness was added. Don't forget also that the gunsight was omitted. The late PR Mk XIX had a bulkhead behind the cockpit which covered the camera bay.

As I was building an early version I needed to put something in the back. A basic frame was built up from square section plastic rod using the access doors in the fuselage sides as a guide. Whilst rummaging through the spares box I found some cameras left over from a Revell 1/32nd scale RF-4E Phantom which fitted nicely in the frame. So they would stand out a bit more the lenses of the cameras were drilled out and some self-adhesive nail art gemstones were inserted. The camera port was drilled out in the fuselage side and a disc of clear plastic glued into the hole. Once set this was sanded flush and polished back to clarity with a four-way nail polishing block. The underside camera ports are actually recessed so their positions were drilled out oversize and two lengths of plastic tube were fixed into the holes, then sanded flush with the surface. The recesses were painted PRU Blue and when dry some clear plastic was put on the inside for the ports. Before closing the fuselage the camera bay and rear cockpit frame were put in position and fixed in place, the majority of the cockpit can be added later through the hole in the bottom of the fuselage.

It was now time to fit the new resin tailfin and Griffon engine. This would involve some more cutting, filling and sanding so it was important to try and seal off the camera bay as much as possible, because any debris that made it onto the inside of the camera port would now be impossible to clean off. The tail fin was fairly straightforward to do but the engine would need a little more work. It is one large heavy piece of resin that would probably put a lot of strain on the undercarriage so I decided to lighten it by drilling into the rear face and removing as much material as I could, messy but worth doing. With the nose in place and the seams all filled and sanded the fuselage panel lines were engraved with the P-Cutter in combination with a straight edge and some Dymo tape as a guide. With the camera bay covering removed, the rest of the cockpit parts were fitted now and the wing and fuselage brought together along with the tailplanes. The radiators were dealt with next and these needed a few bits adding to finish them. There is no attempt at the radiator faces at all, so these were made from pieces of a 1/24th scale car radiator. The movable outlet flaps have to be made up from thin plasticard. Before fitting them to the wings the interiors were painted with the PRU Blue and the radiator faces black, dry-brushed with a dark grey. As with the camera ports this would make masking easier when it came to the painting stage. Another addition unique to the PR Spits were two teardrop fairings on the underside of the wings that overlap onto the undercarriage doors. These house the fuel pumps needed for the additional fuel tanks in the wings. I believe I used two halves of a bomb from a 1/48th scale Spitfire Mk V for these.

The last job on the list before painting was to fit the front and rear cockpit canopy sections. The vacformed canopy provided was not at all good, the frames edges were very vague, the clarity wasn't too good but worst of all, the front screen was the wrong shape. For the rear and sliding hood section you can just use kit parts but for the screen you will need to make something. Luckily this isn't too difficult as all that is needed is some clear sheet and a rod that matches the curvature of the hood. If I remember correctly I used the tail of a drill bit for mine. Heat a strip of clear sheet until it softens and lay it over the rod to get the curvature. Tape the sliding hood in the closed position; you can then use it as a guide to cut your new screen to shape. Once trimmed it was fixed into place with some PVA glue and left to set. With the sliding section removed the cockpit and screens were masked up and given a coat of Interior Grey-Green. The camera ports, radiators and rear wheel bay were all masked up with either Blu Tack or foam and the whole model was given a coat of primer.

Colour

With the primer dry it was time for some paint. As I was building this as an early machine from 1944 there was very little in the way of weathering to do so it was straight on with a coat of Xtracolor X8 BS636 RAF PRU Blue. This was followed by a lot of masking for the invasion stripes. Being a gloss finish I could move straight on to the decals. Most of these were from the spares box with the exception of the tail codes. These should be in grey but after much searching I had to admit defeat and do them in black.

These aircraft seem to have been very well maintained so just a light application of exhaust staining and a few light chips and scratches around the cockpit were added. I could now add the propeller, exhausts and undercarriage before giving the whole model a coat of Vallejo satin clear. Once dry the remaining masking was removed and some oils stains were applied to the underside. With the addition of the sliding canopy and aerials I could call the model finished.

Verdict

I have to say I am pleased with the result but if I were to do another PR Mk XIX I would take a different route. The Hasegawa kit is quite old now and some aspects of the Grey Matter conversion are a little challenging. Add to this the need to add a harness set and a few other bits and pieces a better starting point would be to base the conversion on the Pacific Coast Mk XIV kit. On the plus side, how many of us already have at least one of the Hasegawa kits sitting in the loft?

★ **Lavochkin LaGG-3, 'White 24', Soviet Air Force, 1944**
Dark Grey AMT11 and black Green AMT12 upper surfaces camouflage with Light Blue AMT7 undersides; white '24' on fuselage sides; red stars on fin, red stars with white and red borders on fuselage sides and below wings; no top wing markings; white/black fin/rudder top striping

★ **Lavochkin La-5, 'White 36', Soviet Air Force, 1944/45**
Medium Grey AMT-11 and black Green AMT-112 upper surfaces camouflage with Light Blue AMT-7 undersides; white '36' on fuselage sides; red/white stars (without outer red border) on fuselage sides and fin/rudder only

★ **Lavockin La-5FN, 'White 69', flown by Ladislav Valousek of the 1st Czechoslovakian Fighter Regiment, Proskurov (Ukraine), September 1944**
Medium/Dark Grey upper surfaces with Light Blue undersides; white '69' on fuselage sides; red/white stars on fuselage sides and fin/rudder, plain red below wings

★ **Lavochkin La-7, 'White 23', flown by Maj. V.A. Orekhov, Commander of the 1st Flight, 32nd GFAR, autumn 1944**
Medium Grey AMT-11 and Black Green AMT-112 upper surfaces camouflage with Light Blue AMT-7 undersides; white '23' on fuselage sides outlined in red; red spinner and front of cowling, two white angled bars on fin/rudder; red/white stars on fin/rudder, fuselage sides and underneath wings (no stars on top of wings)

★ **Petlyakov Pe-8, 'Red 6', 25th GvAPPD, Balabasovo, 1945**
Upper surfaces in Dark Green FS.34102, Grey-Brown FS.34201 and black; all black undersides; national markings on fin, fuselage sides and below wings; red '6' on fin thinly outlined in white